KS3 Maths Progress

Confidence • Fluency • Problem-solving • Progression

π ONE

Progression Workbook

Includes videos linked from QR codes!

ALWAYS LEARNING

PEARSON

Contents

Published by Pearson Education Limited, 80 Strand, London, WC2R 0RL

www.pearsonschoolsandfecolleges.co.uk

Text © Pearson Education Limited 2014
Edited by Project One Publishing Solutions and Elektra Media Ltd
Typeset by Elektra Media Ltd
Original illustrations © Pearson Education Limited 2014
Cover illustration by Robert Samuel Hanson

The right of Diane Oliver to be identified as the author of this work has been asserted by her in accordance with the Copyright, Designs and Patents Act 1988.

First published 2014

19
10 9 8 7 6

British Library Cataloguing in Publication Data
A catalogue record for this book is available from the British Library.

ISBN 978 1 447 97111 5

Printed in Slovakia by Neografia

Every effort has been made to contact copyright holders of material reproduced in this book. Any omissions will be rectified in subsequent printings if notice is given to the publishers.

Pearson Education Limited is not responsible for the content of any external internet sites. It is essential for tutors to preview each website before using it in class so as to ensure that the URL is still accurate, relevant and appropriate. We suggest that tutors bookmark useful websites and consider enabling students to access them through the school/college intranet.

1 Real The table shows the number of siblings each student has from a Year 7 class.

Number of siblings	Number of students
0	7
1	14
2	5
3	4
4	1

> **Literacy hint**
> 'Siblings' are your brothers and sisters.

a How many students have no siblings? ....

b How many students have more than 1 sibling? ....

c What is the most common number of siblings? ....

d How many students are in the class altogether? ....

2 This pictogram shows the numbers of phone calls Safiya made.

> A pictogram uses pictures to show data. The key shows what each picture represents.

> **Literacy hint**
> Data is a set of information.

Numbers of calls made

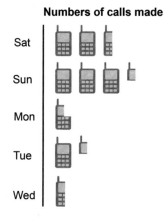

Sat

Sun

Mon

Tue

Wed

Key:  represents 4 phone calls

Day	Calls
Sat	10
Sun	
Mon	
Tue	
Wed	

a How many calls do these represent?

i .... ii ....

b Complete the table to show the number of calls she sent each day.

c On which day did she make the most calls? ....

d How many calls did she make at the weekend?

Guided

10 + ... = ...

> **Literacy hint**
> 'Altogether' means 'add them all up'.

e How many calls did she make altogether?

.... + ... + ... + ... + ... = ...

3 Real This pictogram shows the shoe sizes of some Year 7 girls.

a How many girls have shoe size 6? ....

b What is the most common shoe size? ....

c How many girls have shoe size bigger than 4? ....

d Three girls have shoe size $6\frac{1}{2}$.

Draw the pictures on the diagram to show this.

Y7 girls' shoe sizes

Key: 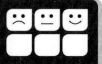 represents 2 girls

CHECK   Tick each box as your **confidence** in this topic improves.

Need extra help? Go to page 7 and tick the boxes next to Q1–4. Then have a go at them once you've finished 1.1–1.6.

1 The bar chart shows the mobile phone covers sold by a shop.

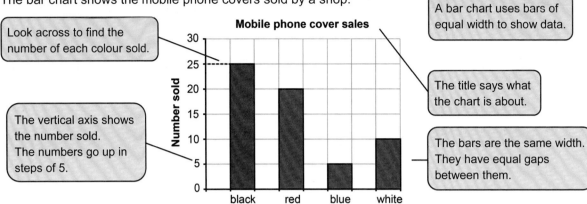

Look across to find the number of each colour sold.

A bar chart uses bars of equal width to show data.

Mobile phone cover sales

The title says what the chart is about.

The vertical axis shows the number sold. The numbers go up in steps of 5.

The bars are the same width. They have equal gaps between them.

a How many of each colour cover were sold?

25 black, 20 red, ...

b More red covers than blue covers were sold. How many more?

20 – .... = ...

c How many covers were sold altogether?

25 + ... + ... + ... = ...

2 The table shows the pets of some Year 7 students. Complete the bar chart.

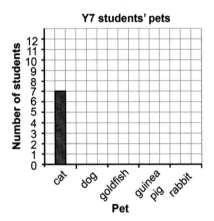

Y7 students' pets

Type of pet	Number of students
cat	7
dog	12
goldfish	3
guinea pig	2
rabbit	3

Worked example

3 The bar-line chart shows the numbers of goals scored by a school netball team in its matches.

A bar-line chart uses lines instead of bars.

a How many times did the team score 6 goals? ....

b Work out the total number of matches that the team played.

Make the bars the same width. Put spaces between the bars. Give your chart a title.

c The team has one final match to play. What is the most likely number of goals it will score?

Which number of goals is the most common?

Write the number of matches for each number of goals. In 2 matches the team scored 2 goals, etc.

CHECK   Tick each box as your **confidence** in this topic improves.

Need extra help? Go to page 8 and tick the box next to Q5. Then have a go at it once you've finished 1.1–1.6.

1 Daisy counted the books in students' school bags.

~~1, 2, 3, 2, 1,~~ 0, 5, 2, 3, 2, 1, 0, 1, 2, 3, 2, 5, 3, 4, 4, 2, 3, 2, 3, 4

a Tally the numbers in the table. Fill in the frequency column.

Books	Tally	Frequency
0		
1	I	
2	II	
3	I	
4	I	
5		
Total		

> Work along the row of numbers.
> Point to one number at a time and tally it.
> Cross off each number as you tally it.

> You can record data in a tally chart.
> Use a tally mark I for each value.
> Group tally marks in 5s like this ⊮

> The frequency is the number of times something happens. A frequency table gives the frequency for each item.

b How many students had 3 books in their bag? ....

c What is the most common number of books in a bag? ....

d How many bags did Daisy check? How did you work it out?

2 Kasim counted the number of characters in his last 20 text messages.

24, 33, 46, 15, 27, 19, 22, 45, 17, 36,

43, 10, 24, 15, 33, 18, 22, 20, 36, 29

Kasim records his results in this grouped frequency table.

a Which class contains

  i 8 characters ....

  ii 20 characters? ....

b Complete the table.

c How many texts are in the group 21–30 characters? ....

Characters	Tally	Frequency
1–10		
11–20		
21–30		
31–40		
41–50		

3 Alfie investigated the number of times each student answered a question in class on Wednesday. He recorded his results in a grouped frequency table.

Number of questions	Frequency
0–4	10
5–9	14
10–14	4
15–19	2

a Which group has the highest frequency?

b Draw a grouped frequency diagram for the data.

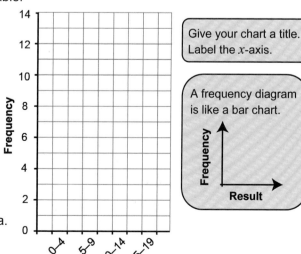

> Give your chart a title. Label the x-axis.

> A frequency diagram is like a bar chart.

CHECK   Tick each box as your **confidence** in this topic improves.

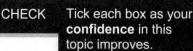

Need extra help? Go to page 8 and tick the box next to Q6. Then have a go at it once you've finished 1.1–1.6.

3

1.4 Mode and modal class

1 Matt is in the school football team.
These are the outcomes of the games he has played in so far this year.

draw, win, draw, lose, win, draw, draw, win, win, draw, draw, win

a Complete the frequency table.

Outcome	Tally	Frequency
win		
draw		
lose		

> **Worked example**
>
>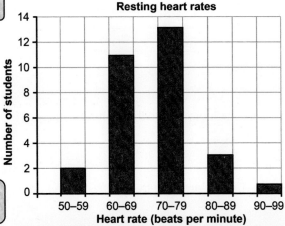

> The mode is the most common item in a set of data. It has the highest frequency.

b What is the mode? ....

2 Write down the mode for each set of values.

> Draw a frequency table.

> **Literacy hint**
> Values can be words, numbers, fractions, decimals, shapes, objects, etc.

a brown, brown, blonde, brown, ginger, brown, brown, blonde, blonde, blonde

b 4, 6, 8, 2, 6, 8, 4, 7, 8, 4, 7, 5, 8, 3, 2

c 0.3 kg, 0.5 kg, 0.2 kg, 0.7 kg, 0.4 kg, 0.1 kg, 0.6 kg, 0.5 kg

3 Katie recorded how many lengths each student swam during a swimming lesson.
The table shows her results.

Lengths	Frequency
1–5	2
6–10	4
11–15	12
16–20	7
21–25	1

> Look for the class with the highest frequency.

> The modal class is the class or group with the highest frequency.

What is the modal class?

 The modal class is .... ← Write the class.

4 Real Jess recorded the resting heart rate of the students in her class.
The frequency diagram shows her results.

a What is the modal class for the heart rate?

b How many students had a resting heart rate between 60 and 79 beats per minute?

> Which bars do you need to look at?

Resting heart rates

(Bar chart: Number of students vs Heart rate (beats per minute))
- 50–59: 2
- 60–69: 11
- 70–79: 13
- 80–89: 3
- 90–99: 1

CHECK Tick each box as your **confidence** in this topic improves.

Need extra help? Go to page 8 and tick the box next to Q7. Then have a go at it once you've finished 1.1–1.6.

1 Order the values from smallest to largest.
Work out their range.

a 4, 2, 7, 6, 5, 4, 8, 5, 6

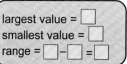

The range shows how spread out a set of data is.

range = largest value − smallest value

b 45, 25, 30, 60, 50, 65, 40

largest value = ☐
smallest value = ☐
range = ☐ − ☐ = ☐

2 Find the median of each set of data.

a 13, 16, 12, 15, 19

median = _____

Write the values in order from smallest to largest.
Count in to the middle.

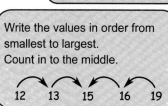

12   13   15   16   19

b 7 m, 4 m, 9 m, 12 m, 6 m, 10 m, 7 m, 10 m, 5 m

The median is the middle value when the data is written in order.

c 24 kg, 56 kg, 30 kg, 45 kg, 28 kg, 50 kg, 33 kg

Don't forget to write the units in your answer.

3 Find the median for each set of data.

a 7, 5, 9, 6, 10, 5

median = _____

b 8, 3, 14, 5, 10, 13

For a data set with an even number of items there are two middle values.
The median is halfway between them.

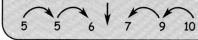

5   5   6   7   9   10

c 41 cm, 24 cm, 27 cm, 46 cm, 30 cm, 40 cm, 28 cm, 45 cm

4 These are the shoe sizes of the girls and boys in Ellie's class.

Girls: 6, 4, 7, 3, 4, 6, 4, 6, 5, 6

Boys: 5, 8, 7, 6, 8, 7, 7, 6, 7, 9

a i Work out the median shoe size for the girls and for the boys.

Worked example

ii Do the boys or the girls have the bigger median shoe size? _____

b Work out the modal shoe size for the girls and for the boys.

c i Work out the range of their shoe sizes.

You can compare two sets of data using the range and the median.

ii Who has the bigger range? _____

CHECK   Tick each box as your **confidence** in this topic improves.

Need extra help? Go to page 8 and tick the boxes next to Q8 and 9. Then have a go at them once you've finished 1.1–1.6.

1 Four friends have these numbers of sweets left.

7, 2, 5, 6

a How many sweets do they have altogether? ....

b They share the sweets equally. How many does each person have? ....

2 Work out the mean for each set of values.

a 4, 6, 7, 8, 10

total = 4 + 6 + 7 + 8 + 10 = ...

mean = ... ÷ 5 = ...

> Add up the values.

> There are 5 values so divide the total by 5.

b 7, 9, 13, 19

c 4, 5, 5, 8, 4, 6, 4, 7, 2

d 12 cm, 43 cm, 26 cm, 33 cm, 37 cm, 29 cm

e 80 g, 60 g, 40 g, 60 g, 50 g, 40 g

> Mode and median are both averages. They show a typical value for a set of data.
> The mean is another average.

> Enter 7 + 9 + 13 + 19
> Press the = key to give the total.
> Enter ÷ 4
> Press the = key to give the mean.

3 Five students raise these amounts for a sponsored silence.

£3, £7, £8, £12, £17

Work out the mean amount collected.

> When dealing with money, 9.4 on a calculator display means £9.40.

Worked example

4 In a science lesson some students measured their weights.

32 kg, 40 kg, 33 kg, 37 kg, 33 kg, 31 kg, 39 kg, 35 kg

Work out

a the median

b the mode

c the mean

d the range.

> The median is the middle value when the data is written in order.

> The mode is the most common item in a set of data.

> range = largest value − smallest value

CHECK   Tick each box as your **confidence** in this topic improves.

Need extra help? Go to page 8 and tick the box next to Q10. Then have a go at it once you've finished 1.1–1.6.

6

1 Strengthen

Tables

☐ 1 Write down the numbers for these tallies.

a ||| ....

b ЖП II ....

c ЖП ЖП I ....

☐ 2 Here are some coins.

a Count each coin. Write the numbers in the table.

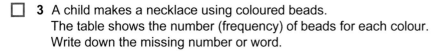

Coin	Number of coins
1p	3
20p	
50p	
£1	

b Which is the most common coin? ....

c How many coins are there altogether?

3 + ... + ... + ... = ...

d What is the total of the numbers in the table? ....

e What do you notice about your answers to **c** and **d**?

☐ 3 A child makes a necklace using coloured beads.
The table shows the number (frequency) of beads for each colour.
Write down the missing number or word.

Colour	Frequency
red	14
blue	12
yellow	19
purple	7

a There are .... red beads.

b There are .... more yellow beads than red beads.

c There are .... beads in total.

d 7 beads are ....

e The most common colour is ....

Charts

☐ 4 Saskia drew a pictogram for the types of biscuits in a tin.

Biscuits in a tin

a Look at the key. Draw the symbols for

i 2 biscuits ....

ii 1 biscuit ....

iii 3 biscuits ....

b How many chocolate biscuits are there? ....

c How many shortbread biscuits are there? ....

d Complete this table.

Biscuit	chocolate	shortbread	ginger	wafer
Frequency				

e Which is the most common biscuit? ....

Key: stands for 2 biscuits

Q4a

 = 2 biscuits  = 1 biscuit

5 A Year 7 class visited the zoo. The bar chart shows what each student chose as their favourite animal.

Y7 favourite animal

a How many students chose the lion? ....

b Which animal was the most popular? ....

c How many students chose the elephant? ....

d How many more students chose the jaguar than the monkey? ....

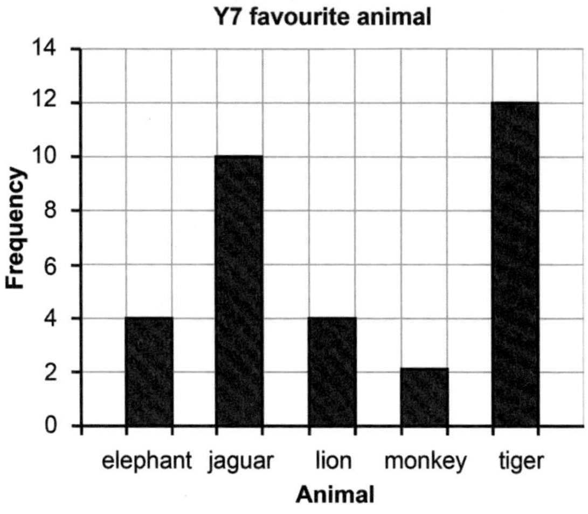

6 Mr Fry recorded how many times his Year 7 English group used the word 'the' in their latest piece of writing.

6, 12, 4, 15, 11, 15, 7, 9, 6, 19,

21, 12, 13, 10, 9, 13, 14, 9, 14, 8

He started this grouped frequency table.

Number of 'the'	Tally	Frequency
0–4	I	1
5–9		
10–14		
15–19		
20–24		

a Complete the grouped frequency table.

b What is the modal class? ....

c Complete the bar chart for his data.

> Which class has the highest frequency?

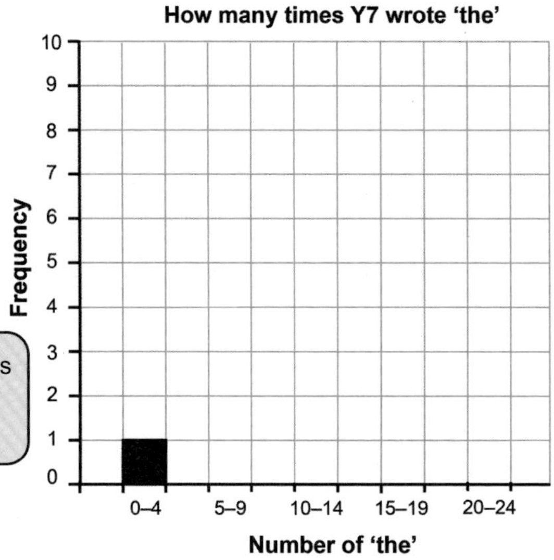

How many times Y7 wrote 'the'

Averages and range

7 Write down the mode of this set of data.

4, 6, 3, 7, 4, 5, 3, 6, 3, 2, 5, 3, 1

> Mode = most common

8 Five Year 7 students estimated the length of this line in centimetres.

_____

5, 9, 3, 10, 8

a What was the smallest estimate? ....

b What was the largest estimate? ....

c Work out the range.

> range = largest value − smallest value

9 Write the estimates from Q8 in order, from smallest to largest. Work out the median.

> Median is the middle value when they are in order.

10 a Add up the estimates from Q8. ....

   b How many estimates are there? ....

   c Work out the mean.

> To find the mean, divide the total by the number of values.

1 Some Year 7 students were asked what type of films they liked watching the most. Draw a pictogram to show the data.

Action	Animation	Comedy	Sci-fi
20	15	45	20

2 Problem-solving The range of the heights of these children is 12 cm. What is the tallest height?

137 cm

3 Reasoning The bar chart shows the numbers of accidents in school reported for Year 7 students in the Autumn term.

a In which month were 15 accidents reported? ....

> The bar height is halfway between 10 and 20 on the scale.

b In which month were there the most accidents? ....

c Work out the range of the number of accidents over the autumn term. ....

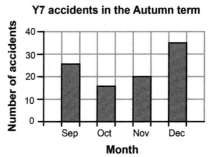

Y7 accidents in the Autumn term

d For two weeks at the start of December there was snow and ice on the ground. There were 35 accidents in December. Do you think the snow and ice made a difference?

4 Real

a A weather station forecasts these maximum monthly temperatures (°C) in Manchester.

6, 8, 11, 11, 15, 19, 22, 24, 16, 13, 14, 5

i Work out the range. ....

ii Find the mode. ....

b The actual maximum temperatures (°C) for each month are shown below.

7, 7, 10, 12, 16, 18, 20, 20, 17, 14, 10, 7

i Work out the range. ....

ii Find the mode. ....

c Compare the actual temperatures with the forecast temperatures using

i the range

ii the mode.

> **Strategy hint**
> The range for the forecast temperatures is .... than for the actual temperatures.

9

5 Reasoning Finn measured the weights of five of his friends.
Each friend has a different weight. The median weight is 34 kg. The range of the weights is 7 kg.
Write if each statement is true or false.

a At least one person is lighter than 34 kg. ....

b One friend is 10 kg heavier than another friend. ....

c The heaviest person is 34 kg + 7 kg. ....

d Two friends weigh 34 kg. ....

6 Reasoning A group of 10 pupils each gave two cakes a score out of 20.

Cake A   16, 14, 17, 13, 15, 16, 13, 19, 14, 16

Cake B   20, 7, 9, 10, 19, 12, 16, 3, 5, 4

Which cake would you recommend and why?

> Compare the ranges and the medians.

7 Reasoning

a Work out the mean of the numbers 10 and 14. ....

b What is the median of 10 and 14? ....

c What do you notice about your answers to **a** and **b**?

> The median of two numbers is the number halfway between them.

d Use the mean to find the median of

   i 34 and 46 ....   ii 5 and 31 ....   iii 25 and 30. ....

8 STEM / Real

a During the winter of 2013–2014, the UK experienced a spell of extreme stormy weather.
These are the monthly rainfall figures (in millimetres) for one of the affected areas from
November to February.

43, 122, 166, 130

   i Work out the median monthly rainfall.

> To find the median of two numbers use the method used in Q7d.

   ii Work out the range of the monthly rainfall.

b These are the rainfall figures for the same four months in the previous year.

139, 134, 80, 32

   i Work out the median monthly rainfall.

   ii Work out the range of the monthly rainfall.

c **Reasoning** Compare the monthly rainfall in 2012–2013 and 2013–2014.
Write a sentence for the median and a sentence for the range.

1 Unit test

> **PROGRESS BAR** Colour in the progress bar as you get questions correct.
> Then fill in the progression chart on pages 111–113.

1 The pictogram shows the favourite sports of some Year 7 boys.

Y7 favourite sports

a How many boys like athletics best? ....

b How many boys like football best? ....

c Seven boys like cricket best.
Draw the symbols on the pictogram to show this.

d How many boys are there altogether? ....

Key: ⊕ represents 4 boys

2 Helen recorded the number of televisions per household
for the students in her class.

3, 2, 1, 2, 2, 1, 2, 3, 4, 2, 3, 4, 2, 1, 3
2, 2, 3, 1, 2, 3, 2, 2, 1, 3, 4, 2, 3, 2, 1

She crossed off the numbers she recorded in this tally chart.

a Complete the tally chart.

b Find the mode. ....

c Which number of televisions has a frequency of 8? ....

d The teacher called out a student's name.
How many televisions is that student's household most likely to have? ....

TVs	Tally	Frequency
1	II	
2	ЖHI	
3	III	
4	I	

3 Miss Smith recorded the test results for her Year 7 class.

a How many students scored 41 to 60?

b Carly scored 57. Which class contains this value?

c Find the modal class.

d The pass mark for the test was 61 marks.
How many students passed the test?

Year 7 test results

4 A group of students from two schools were tested on 20 spellings.

a The students from School A had these results.

15, 12, 9, 17, 14, 12, 16, 19

i Work out the range. ....

ii Find the mode. ....

iii Work out the median. ....

iv Calculate the mean. ....

b The students from School B had these results.

range = 8, mode = 11, median = 13

i Which school had the smaller range? ....

ii Which school achieved the greater modal score? ....

2.1 Adding

1 Work out

   a 30 + 20 + 40 = ...   **b** 40 + 10 + 60 = ...   **c** 50 + 60 + 80 = ...

2 Add each pair of numbers together in your head.

   a 18 + 25 = ...   **b** 26 + 39 = ...

   c 47 + 78 = ...   **d** 87 + 56 = ...

> Split the numbers into tens and units.
> 18 + 25 = ☐
> 10 + 20 + 8 + 5 = ☐

3 Write down the number you need to add to make 100.

   a 64 ....

   64 + 6 = 70

   70 + 30 = 100

   6 + 30 = ...

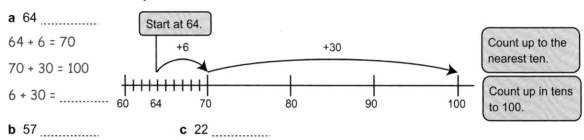

> Start at 64.

> Count up to the nearest ten.

> Count up in tens to 100.

   b 57 ....   **c** 22 ....

4 Work out these additions using the column method.

   a 79 + 85

```
    7 9
  + 8 5
  -------
      4
    1 1
```

> Start in the units column. Add the numbers together (9 + 5 = 14) Put the 4 in the units column and carry the ten. Write the ten as a 1 underneath the tens column.

> Next add the tens (7 tens + 8 tens) and then add the ten carried over. This makes 16 tens.

> In the column method you write the numbers in the calculation in their place value columns. Line up the units with units, and the tens with tens.

   b 58 + 67...............   **c** 97 + 46 ....   **d** 136 + 425 ....   **e** 357 + 258 ....

5 At the end of term some students were given a choice of trips to go on. The table shows how many girls and how many boys chose each trip. Work out the total number of students for each trip.

Trip	Girls	Boys
A	175	86
B	236	158
C	167	437

6 Round each number to the nearest 10.

   a 58 ....

   b 85 ....

   c 144 ....

> Is 58 closer to 50 or 60?
>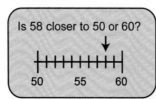
> 50   55   60

> To round to the nearest 10, find the multiple of 10 that the number is closest to. Look at the digit in the units column. If the digit is less than 5, round down. If the digit is 5 or more, round up.

7 Use approximation to estimate these sums.

   a 34 + 58 ≈ ....

   b 28 + 75 ≈ ....

   c 104 + 68 ≈ ....

> An approximation is a number that is not exact. It is close enough for it to be useful though. Use approximations to estimate the answer to calculations. ≈ means 'approximately equal to'.

CHECK   Tick each box as your **confidence** in this topic improves.

Need extra help? Go to page 19 and tick the boxes next to Q1, 2, 3 and 7. Then have a go at them once you've finished 2.1–2.7.

2.2 Subtracting

1 Work out

a 53 – 27

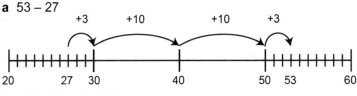

+3   +10   +10   +3

20   27 30   40   50 53   60

3 + 10 + 10 + 3 = 26

53 – 27 = ...

Using a number line start at the lower number (27). Count up to the next number of tens (30). Count up to the number of tens in the higher number (50). Count on to the higher number (53).

You have counted 3, then 10, then 10, then 3.

b 85 – 36 .... **c** 123 – 74 ....

2 Use the column method to work out these.

a 87 – 23 .... **b** 84 – 31 ....

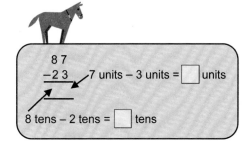

$$\begin{array}{r} 8\,7 \\ -2\,3 \end{array}$$ 7 units – 3 units = ☐ units

8 tens – 2 tens = ☐ tens

3 In your head, subtract each number from 100.

a 42 .... **b** 76 .... **c** 14 ....

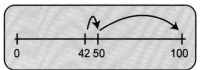

0   42 50   100

4 Use approximation to estimate these calculations.

a 66 – 24 ≈ .... **b** 83 – 38 ≈ .... **c** 147 – 78 ≈ ....

Round each number to the nearest ten and then subtract.

5 Use the column method to work out these.

a 345 – 128

$$\begin{array}{r} 3\,4\,5 \\ -\,1\,2\,8 \\ \hline \end{array}$$

Write the larger number on top.

Start with the units column.
You can't subtract 8 from 5 because this gives a negative answer.

$$\begin{array}{r} 3\ {}^{3}4\ {}^{1}5 \\ -\,1\ \ 2\ \ 8 \\ \hline 7 \end{array}$$

Take a ten from the 4 tens to make 3 tens and 15 units.
15 – 8 = 7

Now look at the tens column and the hundreds column.

Worked example

b 462 – 237 .... **c** 581 – 156 .... **d** 635 – 358 .... **e** 532 – 179 ....

6 Reasoning Sal needs to subtract 48 from 73.
She can't subtract 8 from 3, so she subtracts 3 from 8.
Will she get the right answer? Explain how you know.

$$\begin{array}{r} 7\,3 \\ -\,4\,8 \\ \hline \end{array}$$

Need extra help? Go to page 19 and tick the boxes next to Q4, 5 and 6. Then have a go at them once you've finished 2.1–2.7.

2.3 Multiplying

1 Double these numbers.

   a 14 _____

   b 21 _____

   c 36 _____

> $\begin{array}{c} 14 \\ \times 2 \,\overparen{10 + 4}\, \times 2 \\ \overparen{20 + 8} \\ \hline 28 \end{array}$
>
> Doubling is the same as ×2 (multiplying by 2).

2 Work out

   a 6 × 3 _____

   b 7 × 6 _____

   c 8 × 9 _____

3 Look at these numbers.

4	15	7	10
12	20	13	5

> A multiple is a number that is in a times table.
> 2 × 7 = 14
> 14 is a multiple of 2 and a multiple of 7.

Write down the numbers from the box that are multiples of

   a 2 _____

   b 3 _____

   c 4 _____

   d 5 _____

   e 4 and 5. _____

> **Q3 Strategy hint**
> Learn your times tables so that you don't have to work them out each time.

4 Reasoning Tracy buys 4 bags of donuts with 5 donuts in each bag.
Jayden buys 5 bags of donuts with 4 donuts in each bag.

   a Tick the statement which is true.

      A Tracy has more donuts than Jayden.

      B Jayden has more donuts than Tracy.

      C Tracy and Jayden have the same number of donuts.

   b Explain how you know.

5 Reasoning / Problem-solving There are 30 pupils in a class. They need to get into groups of 4.

   a Is this possible? _____

 Guided

   7 × 4 = _____ , 8 × 4 = _____

   b What size groups will work exactly? _____

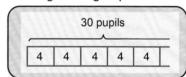

6 Work out

   a 4^2 _____

   b 8^2 _____

   c 10^2 _____

   d 15^2 _____

7 Reasoning Circle the square numbers in the box. Explain how you know.

39	49	144	5	20
81	68	1	16	25

> To find the square of a number you multiply the number by itself.
> For example, 5 squared = 5 × 5 = 25.
> You write 5 squared as 5^2.

> A square root is a number that is multiplied by itself to produce a given number. Finding the square root is the inverse of squaring.
> 5 × 5 = 25, so $\sqrt{25}$ = 5, where $\sqrt{\ }$ means square root.

8 Find the square root of each number using a calculator.

   a 36 _____

   b 16 _____

   c 9 _____

   d 100 _____

   e 144 _____

   f 225 _____

   g 625 _____

   h 25 _____

   i 4489 _____

CHECK Tick each box as your **confidence** in this topic improves.

Need extra help? Go to page 20 and tick the boxes next to Q8, 9 and 10. Then have a go at them once you've finished 2.1–2.7.

1 Use the 2 times table to answer these.

a 6 × 2 = 12, 12 ÷ 2 = ...   b 9 × 2 = ..., ... ÷ 2 = ...

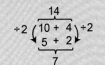

Halving is the same as ÷2 (dividing by 2).

2 Halve each number.

a 14 ....   b 26 ....   c 48 ....   d 54 ....

Halving is the inverse of doubling.

3 Fill in the missing numbers in each sentence.

a Double 10 is 20, so half of 20 is ....

b Double 30 is ...., so half of .... is ....

c Double .... is 34, so half of .... is 17.

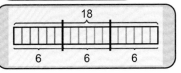

Split the number into tens and units.

Literacy hint
An inverse operation is the opposite operation.

4 Work out

a 18 ÷ 6 = ...

b 24 ÷ 4 = ...   c 20 ÷ 5 = ...

d 42 ÷ 7 = ...   e 24 ÷ 3 = ...

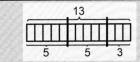

5 Use the multiplication facts to work out the divisions.

a 5 × 4 = 20, so 20 ÷ 5 = ...   b 9 × 12 = 108, so 108 ÷ 9 = ...

c 7 × 8 = 56, so 56 ÷ 8 = ...   d 6 × 11 = 66, so 66 ÷ 11 = ...

Dividing is the inverse of multiplying.
4 × 2 = 8
8 ÷ 2 = 4
8 ÷ 4 = 2

 6 Work out

a 13 ÷ 5 = 2 remainder .... = 2 r ....

b 35 ÷ 4 ....   c 20 ÷ 3 ....

d 40 ÷ 9 ....   e 30 ÷ 7 ....

There are two 5s and 3 left over.

When you can't divide by a number exactly, there is a remainder.

7 Reasoning Alec has 30 chocolates to put into boxes.

a How many rows of 6 can he make? ....

b How many rows of 8 can he make? Are there any left over? ....

8 Reasoning Mollie needs 20 thank you cards.
They come in packs of 8. She says she will need 5 packets.
Is she right? How do you know?

Write a calculation and one sentence to explain.

9 a To estimate 50 ÷ 7

    i round 50 to the nearest number in the 7 times table. ....

    ii work out 49 ÷ 7 = ...

      50 ÷ 7 ≈ ....

28   35   42   (49)   56

b Use the method from part **a** to estimate 70 ÷ 12.

CHECK   Tick each box as your **confidence** in this topic improves.

Need extra help? Go to page 20 and tick the box next to Q11. Then have a go at it once you've finished 2.1–2.7.

1 Multiply each number by 10.

a 6 .... **b** 48 ....

c 228 .... **d** 647 ....

> Multiplying by 10 moves the digits 1 place to the left.
> Multiplying by 100 moves the digits 2 places to the left.
> Multiplying by 1000 moves the digits 3 places to the left.

2 Multiply each number by 100.

a 8 .... **b** 61 .... **c** 85 .... **d** 932 ....

3 Multiply each number by 1000.

a 9 .... **b** 25 .... **c** 73 .... **d** 481 ....

4 Divide each number by 10.

a 50 .... **b** 90 ....

c 180 .... **d** 600 ....

> Dividing by 10 moves the digits 1 place to the right.
> Dividing by 100 moves the digits 2 places to the right.
> Dividing by 1000 moves the digits 3 places to the right.

5 Divide each number by 100.

a 300 .... **b** 700 .... **c** 1900 .... **d** 3000 ....

6 Divide each number by 1000.

a 8000 .... **b** 24 000 .... **c** 52 000 .... **d** 5000 ....

7 Work out these calculations.

$700 \times 100 =$ .... $700 \div 10 =$ ....

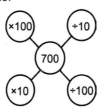

8 There are 1000 g in one kilogram. How many grams are there in

a 4 kilograms ....

b 9 kilograms? ....

	4 kilograms		
1000 g			

9 **STEM / Real** A microscope makes objects look 10 times bigger than in real life.
Part of an object is 3 mm long. How long does it look under the microscope?

10 Work out the mean of these numbers.

9, 8, 11, 6, 12, 14, 7, 9, 6, 8

11 **Reasoning** Complete these.

a $10^2 =$ ...., so $\sqrt{100} =$ .... **b** $100^2 =$ ...., so $\sqrt{\rule{2cm}{0pt}} = 100$

CHECK Tick each box as your **confidence** in this topic improves.

Need extra help? Go to page 20 and tick the boxes next to Q12 and 13. Then have a go at them once you've finished 2.1–2.7.

1 **Reasoning**   Work out the missing numbers in these calculations.

a 24 + _____ = 37   b _____ − 42 = 15

c 6 × _____ = 42   d _____ ÷ 4 = 9

> The four operations are add (+), subtract (−), multiply (×) and divide (÷).

2 Reece and Theia run a biscuit stall to raise money for charity.

a One biscuit costs 15p. What is the total cost of 4 biscuits? _____

b On Wednesday, 4 students buy 12 biscuits and share them equally.
  How many biscuits does each student have?

c On Thursday, they start with 40 biscuits. They sell 31 biscuits.
  How many biscuits do they have left?

d On Friday, Safia buys 3 biscuits and Andre buys 5 biscuits.
  How many biscuits do they buy altogether? .

> In a word problem, you need to work out which operation to use. Look for key words in the question.
> 'Each' often means divide.
> 'Total' or 'altogether' often mean you add or multiply.
> 'Left' often means subtract.

3 How many days are there in

a 4 weeks _____   b 6 weeks _____   c 9 weeks? _____

4 Two sisters share some money. Chloe gets £4 for every £3 that Jenna gets. They share £35.
  How much do they get each?

£4 + £3 = £7 ———
£35 ÷ £7 = _____ ———
Chloe: _____ × £4 = _____
Jenna: _____ × £3 = _____

> Add the two amounts together.

> Multiply Chloe's share by the number of £5.
> Do the same for Jenna.

> Work out the number of £7 in £35.
> £35
> | £4 | £3 | £4 | £3 | £4 | £3 |
> £7   £7   £7

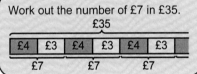

5 In a class there are 2 boys for every 3 girls.
  There are 30 pupils in the class.
  Work out the number of boys and the number of girls.

6 A greengrocer's shop sells 7 apples for every 3 bananas.
  On Monday 90 apples and bananas are sold.
  Work out how many apples are sold and how many bananas are sold.

7 A bag contains 8 satsumas. Each satsuma costs 22p.
  How much does the bag of satsumas cost?

CHECK   Tick each box as your **confidence** in this topic improves.

Need extra help? Go to page 20 and tick the box next to Q14. Then have a go at it once you've finished 2.1–2.7.

17

1 Find the new temperatures.

> **Guided**

a The temperature is –1 °C. It increases by 5 °C. ....

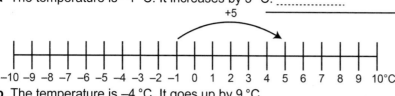

> Use a number line.
> Start at –1 °C. Count up 5 °C.

Literacy hint
'Rise', 'increase' and 'go up' all mean the same thing.

b The temperature is –4 °C. It goes up by 9 °C. ....

c The temperature is –6 °C. It rises by 10 °C. ....

Literacy hint
'Decrease', 'fall' and 'go down' all mean the same thing.

2 Find the new temperatures.

A temperature decrease means you need to subtract the second number from the first.
Use the temperature scale. Start at 5 °C and count back 7 °C.

a The temperature is 5 °C. It decreases by 7 °C. ....

b The temperature is 2 °C. It falls by 10 °C. ....

3 Write the correct symbol, < or >, between each pair of temperatures.

a 4 °C .... 7 °C   **b** 9 °C .... 2 °C   **c** –3 °C .... 2 °C

d 6 °C .... –8 °C   **e** –1 °C .... –4 °C   **f** –6 °C .... –3 °C

The symbol > means greater than.
'6 > 1' means '6 is greater than 1'.
The symbol < means less than.
'–3 < –1' means '–3 is less than –1'.
Use the temperature scale in Q2 to help you.

4 Write the correct symbol, < or >, between each pair of numbers.

a 3 5   **b** 8 3   **c** –4 1

d –2 5   **e** –5 .... –9   **f** –5 .... –1

5 Find the next three numbers in each sequence.

> **Guided**

a 10, 6, 2, ..., ..., ...

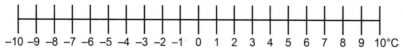

Circle the numbers on a number line.
Count down to find the size of each step.
Count down in the same size steps to find the next three numbers in the sequence.

b 10, 7, 4, ..., ..., ...

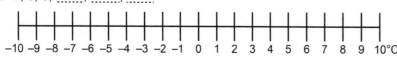

c 7, 5, 3, ..., ..., ...

6 Arrange the numbers in order of size, smallest first.

5, 13, –2, 1, –14, 0, –6, –10 ....

CHECK   Tick each box as your **confidence** in this topic improves.

Need extra help? Go to page 20 and tick the boxes next to Q15–18. Then have a go at them once you've finished 2.1–2.7.

2 Strengthen

Adding and subtracting

☐ **1** Work out

a 36 + 53 .... **b** 51 + 47 .... **c** 75 + 24 ....

= 30 + 50 + 6 + 3 = ...

Split the number into tens and units.

☐ **2** Work out

a 47 + 38 .... **b** 59 + 34 .... **c** 46 + 27 ....

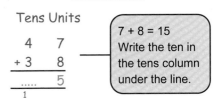

Tens Units

```
    4   7
+   3   8
-----------
    ....  5
    1
```

7 + 8 = 15
Write the ten in the tens column under the line.

d 57 + 49 .... **e** 66 + 47 .... **f** 74 + 58 ....

☐ **3** Work out

a 236 + 425 .... **b** 358 + 574 .... **c** 536 + 67 ....

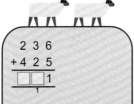

```
  2 3 6
+ 4 2 5
-------
□ □ 1
  1
```

Line up the hundreds, tens and units. Remember to add the carry number.

☐ **4** Work out

a 65 – 41 ....
b 57 – 23 ....
c 79 – 38 ....

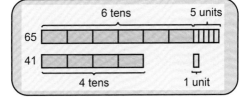

6 tens   5 units
65
41
4 tens   1 unit

☐ **5** Work out

a 41 – 25 ....
b 65 – 38 ....
c 87 – 49 ....

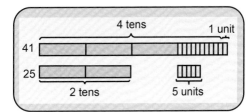

4 tens   1 unit
41
25
2 tens   5 units

☐ **6** Work out

a 256 – 141 .... **b** 354 – 147 .... **c** 346 – 89 ....

☐ **7** Write down the number you need to add to each number to make 100.

a 54 .... **b** 72 ....

c 38 .... **d** 47 ....

Use number lines to help you.

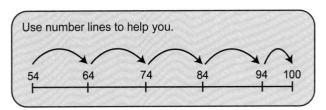

54   64   74   84   94   100

Multiplying and dividing

☐ **8** Draw a diagram to help you work out these multiplications.

    a 3×6 _____

    b 6×5 _____

    c 4×7 _____

    d 6×8 _____

☐ **9** Work out these square numbers.

    a 3^2 _____

    b 4^2 _____

    c 2^2 _____

    d 6^2 _____

☐ **10** Use the given multiplication facts to answer the division questions.

    a $3 \times 7 = 21$. What is $21 \div 7$? _____

    b $6 \times 9 = 54$. What is $54 \div 6$? _____

☐ **11** Work out

    a $16 \div 3$ _____

    b $27 \div 5$ _____

    c $45 \div 8$ _____

> Count in 3s until you get close to 16.
>
> ① ② ③ ④ ⑤
>
> 3, 6, 9, 12, 15
> How many 3s?
> What is the remainder?

☐ **12** Use the place-value table to do these calculations.

    a $6 \times 10 =$ _____

    b $14 \times 100 =$ _____

    c $3 \times 1000 =$ _____

☐ **13** Use the place-value table to do these calculations.

    a $400 \div 100 =$ _____

    b $370 \div 10 =$ _____

    c $70\,000 \div 100 =$ _____

Th	H	T	U

Number skills

☐ **14** In every packet of sweets there are 3 red ones. How many red ones are there in

    a 2 packets _____

    b 5 packets? _____

> 2 packets
> 1 packet
> 3 red sweets | 3 red sweets

☐ **15** Use the thermometer to find the new temperature after these changes.

    a 2°C rises by 5°C _____

    b −4°C rises by 7°C _____

> Start at 2°C. Count up 5.

Rise in temperature

☐ **16** Use the thermometer to find the new temperature after these changes.

    a 2°C falls by 5°C _____

    b 5°C falls by 12°C _____

☐ **17** Write the correct symbol, < or >, between each pair of numbers.

    a 4 _____ 7

    b −2 _____ −6

    c −9 _____ −1

    d −5 _____ 4

> Use the thermometer to help you.
> Put the bigger end of the symbol next to the bigger number, e.g. 5 > 4 and −6 < 5.

Fall in temperature

☐ **18** Write each set of numbers in order, smallest first.

    a 4, −6, 7, −2, 0, 5, −5 _____

    b −3, −8, 4, 8, 1, −10, −1 _____

> **Strategy hint**
> Which is smallest?
> Write it down.
> Cross it off the list.
> Repeat.

+10, +9, +8, +7, +6, +5, +4, +3, +2, +1, 0°C, −1, −2, −3, −4, −5, −6, −7, −8, −9, −10

1 Work out

   a 9^2 ....   **b** 24^2 ....   **c** 37^2 ....

> A small 2 means 'squared'.
> Use the x^2 key.

2 Add each set of numbers in your head.

   a 6, 8, 5, 4, 2, 9 ....   **b** 23, 18, 25, 17, 12 ....

   c 7, 18, 13, 22 ....   **d** 34, 15, 27, 34, 23 ....

> Look for
> • pairs of numbers that make useful totals
> • repeated numbers.

3 Declan owns an ice cream van. The table shows his sales during one week.

	Mon	Tues	Wed	Thur	Fri	Sat	Sun
Ice cream cones	24	21	27	36	41	84	93
Ice cream tubs	13	19	14	12	16	23	27
Ice lollies	18	16	19	25	19	26	34

   a How many more ice cream cones does he sell on Saturday than on Monday? ....

   b What is the difference between the largest and smallest numbers of ice lollies he sells? ....

> largest number   smallest number
> of ice lollies   −   of ice lollies   = ☐

   c What is the difference between the largest and smallest numbers of ice cream tubs he sells? ....

4 Crisps are sold in 25 g bags.
   Each bag of crisps contains 13 g of carbohydrate.
   How much carbohydrate is there in a 175 g bag?

   $175 \div 25 =$ ....

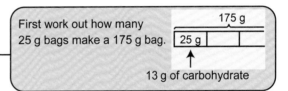

> First work out how many
> 25 g bags make a 175 g bag.
>
> 175 g
> 25 g
>
> 13 g of carbohydrate

5 **Problem-solving** Jake rounds a number to the nearest 10 and gets 370.
   What numbers might Jake have been rounding?

6 Write down the change from £1 when you spend

   a 35p ....   **b** 71p ....   **c** 94p ....

> There are 100p in £1.

7 Chris has 342 dinosaur stickers. 67 of them are dinosaurs from the Triassic period.
   154 are from the Cretaceous period. The rest are from the Jurassic period.
   How many dinosaur stickers are from the Jurassic period?

8 What do you need to add to each of these numbers to make 1000?

   a 570 ....   **b** 80 ....   **c** 348 ....   **d** 841 ....

9 Kyle had £100. He has spent £79.
   How much is left?

10 **Real** A weather station in Barrow, Alaska, recorded these average minimum temperatures during six months in 2012.

Month	Nov	Dec	Jan	Feb	Mar	Apr
Temperature (°C)	−5	−14	−20	−21	−19	−5

Start at the coldest and count up to the warmest.

a Write the temperatures in order, coldest first. ....

b What is the difference in °C between the coldest and warmest months? ....

c In May the average minimum temperature increased by 14 °C.

What was the temperature in May? ....

11 Work out the area of a square with side length

a 3 cm .... b 12 mm .... c 20 m ....

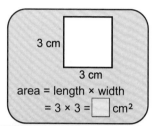

3 cm

3 cm

area = length × width

= 3 × 3 = ☐ cm²

12 **Finance** The largest denomination bank note in Switzerland is 1000 Swiss francs.

a How many of these notes make 30 000 Swiss francs?

The largest denomination bank note means the bank note with the highest face value.

b How much are 24 notes worth?

13 8 kilometres = 5 miles

a Jess walks 16 km. How far is this in miles?

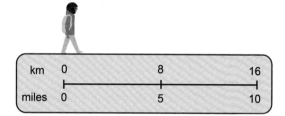

b A coach travels 60 miles to Manchester. How far is this in kilometres?

c Which is further, 30 miles or 45 km?

14 Work out the side length of a square with area

a 144 cm² .... b 729 mm² .... c 7056 m² ....

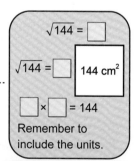

$\sqrt{144}$ = ☐

$\sqrt{144}$ = ☐   144 cm²

☐ × ☐ = 144

Remember to include the units.

15 Use the multiplication facts to help you find the missing numbers.

a 13 × 17 = 221, so 221 ÷ 17 = ...

b 24 × 33 = 792, so 792 ÷ 24 = ...

c 245 × 31 = 7595, so 7595 ÷ 245 = ...

Dividing is the inverse of multiplying.

16 In a school, 5 students wear black trousers for every 3 students who wear grey trousers. There are 272 students in the school.

a How many students wear black trousers?

b How many students wear grey trousers?

2 Unit test

PROGRESS BAR Colour in the progress bar as you get questions correct. Then fill in the progression chart on pages 111–113.

1 Add the numbers in each set.

   a 40, 50, 70 ....   **b** 6, 8, 1, 2, 4 ....

2 Find the new temperatures.

   a The temperature is –4 °C. It rises by 9 °C. ....

   b The temperature is 3 °C. It falls by 6 °C. ....

3 Write down the next three numbers in this sequence. 28, 22, 16, 10, ..., ..., ...

4 Circle the multiples of 4.   11   12   18   20   22   24

5 Ayesha puts chocolates into boxes. For every white chocolate, she adds 4 milk chocolates. In a box of 30 chocolates

   a how many white chocolates are there ....

   b how many milk chocolates are there? ....

6 Add these numbers together.

   a 53 + 45 ....   **b** 67 + 28 ....   **c** 273 + 649 ....   **d** 45 + 38 + 23 ....

7 Work out

   a 76 – 32 ....   **b** 82 – 46 ....   **c** 264 – 87 ....   **d** 741 – 563 ....

8 Use approximation to estimate these calculations.

   a 52 + 68 ....   **b** 86 – 23 ....

9 What do you need to add to 28 to make 100? ....

10 Write these temperatures in order, coldest first.

   –2 °C, 4 °C, –7 °C, 0 °C, 2 °C, –3 °C, –9 °C ....

11 Work out 6^2. ....

12 Work out

   a 57 × 10 ....   **b** 690 ÷ 10 ....   **c** 73 × 100 ....

   b 34 × 1000 ....   **e** 4500 × 100 ....   **f** 18 000 ÷ 1000 ....

13 A café makes a crushed ice drink by mixing 2 litres of juice with 5 litres of water. One day the café sells 35 litres of the crushed ice drink.

   a How much juice have they used? ....

   b How much water have they used? ....

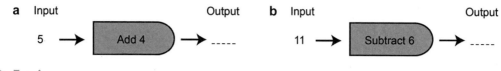

MASTER 3.1 Using functions

1 Work out the outputs of these function machines.

a Input → Add 4 → Output: 5 → .....

5 + 4 = ...

b Input: 11 → Subtract 6 → Output: .....

c Input: 3 → Multiply by 7 → Output: .....

d Input: 20 → Divide by 5 → Output: .....

> A function is a relationship between two sets of numbers. The numbers that go into a function machine are called the input. The numbers that come out are called the output.

2 Work out the outputs of these function machines.

a Input: 12, 16, 20 → − 3 → Output: ....., ..., ...

b Input: 3, 4, 5 → + 7 → Output: 10, ..., ...

c Input: 12, 20, 32 → ÷ 4 → Output: ....., ..., ...

d Input: 3, 5, 9 → × 3 → Output: ....., ..., ...

> Work out
> 3 + 7
> 4 + 7
> 5 + 7

3 a Work out the missing outputs of this function machine.

b Complete the table to show the inputs and outputs of the function machine.

Input	1	3	6	10
Output	9			

Input: 1, 3, 6, 10 → + 8 → Output: 9, ..., ..., ...

4 Complete the table to show the inputs and outputs of the function machine.

Input	2	5	7	10
Output				

Input: 2, 5, 7, 10 → × 2 → Output: ....., ..., ..., ...

5 Real A food chain pays its staff £6.50 per hour.

a Use the function machine to work out how much the staff get paid for shifts of

i 5 hours .... **ii** 7 hours ....

iii 8 hours .... **iv** 10 hours. ....

b Complete the table to show all the inputs and outputs.

Input (hours)	5	7	8	10
Output (£)				

> In a function machine, every input gives an output.

Input: 5, 7, 8, 10 → × 6.5 → Output: ....., ..., ..., ...

CHECK Tick each box as your **confidence** in this topic improves.

Need extra help? Go to pages 30–31 and tick the boxes next to Q5 and 6. Then have a go at them once you've finished 3.1–3.6.

24

1 Write down the missing function for each function machine.

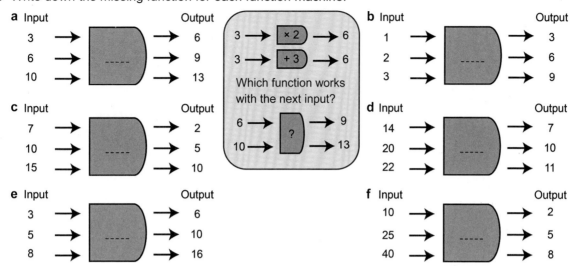

a Input → [-----] → Output
3 → 6
6 → 9
10 → 13

3 → (× 2) → 6
3 → (+ 3) → 6
Which function works with the next input?
6 → [?] → 9
10 → → 13

b Input → [-----] → Output
1 → 3
2 → 6
3 → 9

c Input → [-----] → Output
7 → 2
10 → 5
15 → 10

d Input → [-----] → Output
14 → 7
20 → 10
22 → 11

e Input → [-----] → Output
3 → 6
5 → 10
8 → 16

f Input → [-----] → Output
10 → 2
25 → 5
40 → 8

2 A chef looks at some recipes to see how much pasta is used for the given number of people. The table below shows the values he finds.

Number of people	2	4	10
Amount of pasta (g)	140	280	700

He writes the values on a function machine.

Input → [-----] → Output
2 → 140
4 → 280
10 → 700

a Write down the missing function on the function machine.

b How much pasta should the chef cook per person? ....

c How much pasta should the chef cook for 5 people? ....

Literacy hint
'per person' means 'for each person'.

3 Problem-solving Work out the missing output of this function machine.

Input → [-----] → Output
24 → 4
42 → 7
54 → -----

Work out the function first.

4 Problem-solving Complete this table using the outputs and functions from the cards.

Input	Function	Output
31		
9		
11		
24		

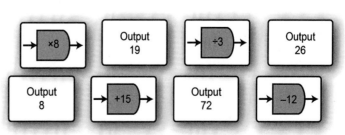

→ (×8) →   Output 19   → (÷3) →   Output 26

Output 8   → (+15) →   Output 72   → (−12) →

CHECK Tick each box as your **confidence** in this topic improves.

Need extra help? Go to page 30 and tick the boxes next to Q3 and 4. Then have a go at them once you've finished 3.1–3.6.

3.3 Simplifying expressions

1 Simplify

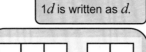
1*d* is written as *d*.

  a $d + d$ ....

  b $3c + 2c$ ....

  c $3x + 4x$ ....

  d $2y + 5y$ ....

  e $2j + 4j$ ....

  f $4k + 2k + k$ ....

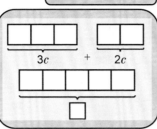

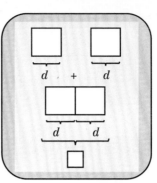

2 Problem-solving Write three additions that simplify to 10*e*.

In maths, if you do not know a value, you can use a letter to represent it.

$\square e + \square e = 10e$

3 Simplify

  a $5m - 2m$ ....

  b $10n - 3n$ ....

  c $9p - 5p$ ....

  d $6q - 2q$ ....

  e $15r - 7r$ ....

  f $5t - t$ ....

$\underbrace{\bigcirc\bigcirc\bigcirc\bigcirc\bigcirc}_{5m} - \underbrace{\bigcirc\bigcirc}_{2m} = \underbrace{\bigcirc\bigcirc\bigcirc}_{\square}$

4 Simplify

 Guided

  a $3w + 4w - 2w$ ....

  $3w + 4w - 2w$

  $= 7w - 2w =$ ....

Work from left to right.
First work out $3w + 4w$, then subtract $2w$.

Worked example

  b $6a - a + 3a$ ....   **c** $12g - 5g + 2g$ ....

  d $15h - 9h + h$ ....   **e** $8s + 7s - 9s$ ....

5 Reasoning   The four cards each show an expression.

  | $4x$ | | $7x - 2x$ | | $9x - 4x$ | | $12x$ |

An expression contains numbers and letters.

  Jack chooses these two cards and adds the expressions. | $7x - 2x$ | | $12x$ |

  $7x - 2x + 12x = 5x + 12x$

  $\qquad\qquad = 17x$

  a Choose two other cards and add the expressions. ....

  b Choose two different cards and add the expressions. ....

  c What is the greatest total you can get by adding the expressions from two cards?
     Show how you worked out your answer.

CHECK   Tick each box as your
confidence in this
topic improves.   ☹ 😐 🙂
☐ ☐ ☐

Need extra help? Go to pages 30–31 and
tick the boxes next to Q5 and 6. Then have a
go at them once you've finished 3.1–3.6.

3.4 Writing expressions

1 Dave knows the white pipe is 12 cm longer than the grey pipe.

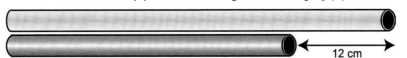

12 cm

Write down how to work out the length of the white pipe.

You write an expression by using letters to stand for numbers.

2 Amy has p pencils. Write an expression for the number of pencils each of these people have.

a Jane has 3 more pencils than Amy. ....

b Tom has 8 more pencils than Amy. ....

c Dan has 2 fewer pencils than Amy. ....

d Becky has 5 fewer pencils than Amy. ....

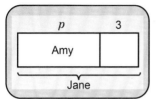

	p	3
	Amy	

Jane

3 a i Complete this function machine to write an expression for 4 more than x.

Input   Output

x → $+4$ → $x +$ _____

'4 more than x' means $x + 4$

ii Use the function machine to work out the output when $x = 12$. ....

Substitute 12 for x, then work out $12 + 4$.

b i Complete this function machine to write an expression for 8 less than t.

Input   Output

t → -8 → _____

Literacy hint
'Substitute' means replace.

ii Use the function machine to work out the output when $t = 15$. ....

4 Emma works for h hours. Kyle works for 3 times as long as Emma.

a Write an expression for how long Kyle works.

Kyle: $h \times 3 =$ ....

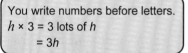

You write numbers before letters.
$h \times 3 = 3$ lots of h
$= 3h$

b Emma works for 2 hours. How long does Kyle work for?

Kyle: $2 \times 3 =$ ....

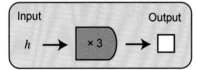

Input   Output

h → $\times 3$ → ☐

5 Problem-solving In a Year 7 class, there are twice as many students who prefer to play games on a tablet than on a smartphone. There are 3 times as many who prefer to play games on a console than on a tablet.
There are g students who prefer to play games on a smartphone.
Write an expression in terms of g for the number of students who prefer to play games on a console.

Worked example

Smartphone   Tablet

g	g	g

6 Match each description to the correct expression.

subtract x from 5	multiply x by 5 then add 5	x subtract 5	multiply x by 5	x add 5

$5x + 5$	$5 - x$	$5x$	$x + 5$	$x - 5$

CHECK Tick each box as your **confidence** in this topic improves.

Need extra help? Go to page 31 and tick the box next to Q7. Then have a go at it once you've finished 3.1–3.6.

1 STEM   The formula to work out the pressure when the force is applied to an area of 7 cm² is

pressure = force ÷ 7

Work out the pressure when the force is 35.

Guided

pressure = force ÷ 7 | Write the formula first. |

= 35 ÷ 7

= .... | Substitute the value for the force into the formula. |

> A formula shows the relationship between different quantities.
> You can write a formula using letters to stand for quantities.
> A formula always has an equals sign '='.

2 STEM   The formula to work out the voltage (V) needed to charge a phone is

$V = 5 \times$ resistance

Find the voltage needed when the resistance is

a 3 ....   **b** 4 ....   **c** 5. ....

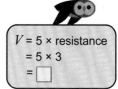

> $V = 5 \times$ resistance
> $= 5 \times 3$
> $= \square$

3 STEM   The table shows the melting points of five metals.

Name of metal	copper	lead	plutonium	sodium	tin
Melting point (°C)	1085	327.5	639.4	97.7	231.9

a Write down the melting points in order, starting with the lowest.

b Work out the range of the melting points. ....

> The formula to work out the range of a set of data is
> range = highest value – lowest value

4 STEM   The formula to work out the average speed of a car when you know the distance it travels and the time taken is

$s = d \div t$

a What do you think the letters d, s and t stand for?

b Complete the workings to find the average speed when

i $d = 70$ and $t = 2$ **ii** $d = 120$ and $t = 3$

Guided

$s = d \div t$ $s = d \div t$

$= 70 \div 2$ $= ....$

$= ....$ $= ....$

5 STEM   The formula to convert centimetres to metres is $M = C \div 100$

a What do you think M and C stand for?

b Use the formula to work out the number of metres when

i $C = 400$ ....   **ii** $C = 160$ ....   **iii** $C = 427$. ....

CHECK   Tick each box as your **confidence** in this topic improves.

Need extra help? Go to page 31 and tick the boxes next to Q8, 9, and 10. Then have a go at them once you've finished 3.1–3.6.

1 Every day a florist makes 7 more bouquets than have been ordered.

You can write a formula to work out an amount in words, then use letters to represent the quantities.

a Write a formula in words for the number of bouquets she makes each day.

number of bouquets made = number of bouquets ordered + ...

b Write a formula that connects the number of bouquets made, m, to the number of bouquets ordered, b.

m = ...

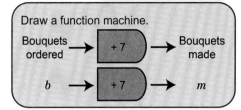

Draw a function machine.

Bouquets ordered → +7 → Bouquets made

b → +7 → m

2 All items in a sale are reduced by £15.

a Work out the sale price of items when the original price is

i £40 .... **ii** £50 .... **iii** £100 ....

b Complete this word formula for the sale price of an item.

sale price = ... – ....

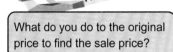

What do you do to the original price to find the sale price?

c Complete this formula that connects the sale price of an item, a, and the original price of the item, b.

a = ... – ....

3 Josie earns £12 per hour. Write a formula that connects the money Josie earns, m, to the hours she works, h.

number of hours × 12 = money Josie earns

h × 12 = ...

m = ...

Rearrange and simplify the formula.

Write the formula in words or as a function machine.

Literacy hint
'Per' means 'for each'.

4 There are 11 players in a football team.

a Complete these.

1 team = 11 players

2 teams = 2 × 11 = ... players

3 teams = 3 × 11 = ... players

t teams = t × 11 = ... players

b Write down the missing function for this machine.

Number of teams → .... → Total number of players

c Write a formula to work out the total number of players, p, when you know the number of teams, t.

5 To make cupcakes you need 14 grams of flour per cake.

a Complete this function machine.

Number of cupcakes → .... → Total amount of flour

b Write a formula to work out the amount of flour, f, you use when you know the number of cupcakes, c.

CHECK Tick each box as your **confidence** in this topic improves.

Need extra help? Go to page 31 and tick the box next to Q11. Then have a go at it once you've finished 3.1–3.6.

3 Strengthen

Functions

1 Work out the outputs of these function machines.

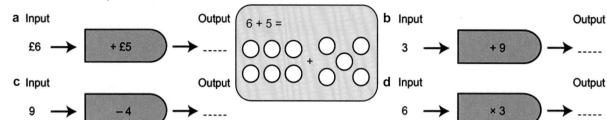

a Input £6 → + £5 → Output -----

6 + 5 =

b Input 3 → + 9 → Output -----

c Input 9 → − 4 → Output -----

d Input 6 → × 3 → Output -----

2 Work out the outputs of these function machines.

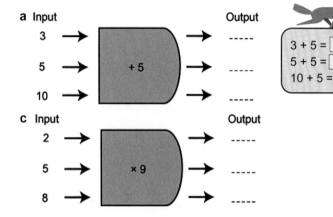

a Input 3 →, 5 →, 10 → + 5 → Output -----, -----, -----

3 + 5 = ☐
5 + 5 = ☐
10 + 5 = ☐

b Input 8 →, 15 →, 19 → − 7 → Output -----, -----, -----

c Input 2 →, 5 →, 8 → × 9 → Output -----, -----, -----

d Input 8 →, 16 →, 20 → ÷ 2 → Output -----, -----, -----

3 Follow these steps to find the function for this machine.

Input 4 →, 7 →, 9 → ? → Output 12, 21, 27

a What are the possible functions for the first input and output?

4 + 8 = 12   4 × .... = 12

b Try both possible functions for 7 → ? → 21.

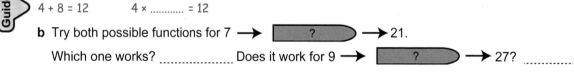

Which one works? .... Does it work for 9 → ? → 27? ....

c Write the function that works for all the inputs and outputs. ....

4 Work out the function for each machine.

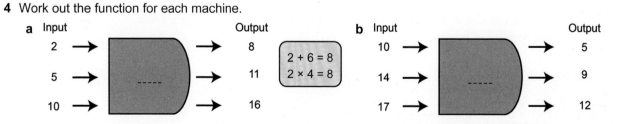

a Input 2 →, 5 →, 10 → ----- → Output 8, 11, 16

2 + 6 = 8
2 × 4 = 8

b Input 10 →, 14 →, 17 → ----- → Output 5, 9, 12

Expressions

1 apple + 1 apple
= ☐ apples
☐ a + ☐ a = ☐ a

5 Simplify

a $a + a$ ....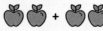

b $a + a + a$ ....

c $2a + 3a$ ....

d $4a + a$ ....

6 Simplify

a $3a - a$ ....

b $5a - 2a$ ....

c $6a - a - 3a$ ....

d $7a - 3a$ ....

3 apples – 1 apple = ☐ apples

$3a \quad - \quad a \quad = \boxed{} \, a$

7 Write the letter to match each statement to its calculation.

| **A** 5×3 | **B** $x - 2$ | **C** $2x$ | **D** $5 + 3$ | **E** $5 - 3$ |

...... Shane has 5 marbles. He buys 3 more.

...... Clare has x texts. She deletes 2.

...... Zach has 5 sweets. Katie has three times as many.

...... Kira has 5 chocolates. She eats 3.

...... Paul has x pens. Lara has twice as many.

Worked example

Formulae

8 Complete the workings using the formula $M = N + 4$ to work out the value of M when

a $N = 5$

$M = N + 4 = 5 + 4 =$ ....

b $N = 8$

$M = N + 4 = 8 + 4 =$ ....

c $N = 3$

$M = N + 4 =$ .... $+ 4 =$ ....

d $N = 16$

$M = N + 4 =$ .... $+$ .... $=$ ....

9 Complete the workings using the formula $D = E + F$ to work out the value of D when

a $E = 5$ and $F = 7$

$D = E + F = 5 + 7 =$ ....

b $E = 3$ and $F = 8$

$D = E + F = 3 + 8 =$ ....

c $E = 12$ and $F = 9$

$D = E + F =$ .... $+$ .... $=$ ....

d $E = 11$ and $F = 15$

$D = E + F =$ .... $+$ .... $=$ ....

10 Complete the workings using the formula $S = 8T$ to work out the value of S when

a $T = 3$

$S = 8T = 8 \times 3 =$ ....

b $T = 5$

$S = 8T = 8 \times 5 =$ ....

$8T$ means $8 \times T$

c $T = 7$

$S = 8T = 8 \times$ .... $=$ ....

d $T = 12$

$S = 8T =$ .... $\times$ .... $=$ ....

11 In a football match, Team A won by 2 more goals than Team B.

a What is the function? ....

b Team B scored 3 goals. How many goals did Team A score? ....

c Complete the function machine.

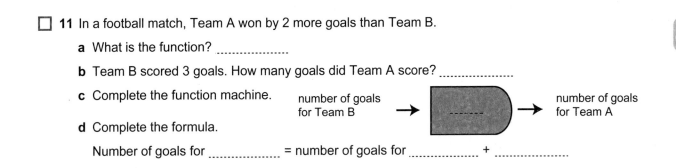

number of goals for Team B → [..........] → number of goals for Team A

d Complete the formula.

Number of goals for .... = number of goals for .... + ...

3 Extend

1 Work out the missing inputs and outputs of these function machines.

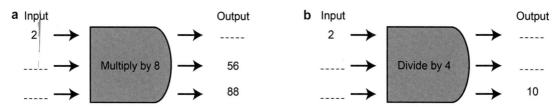

a Input → Multiply by 8 → Output
2 → → -----
----- → → 56
----- → → 88

b Input → Divide by 4 → Output
2 → → -----
----- → → -----
----- → → 10

2 Problem-solving   Use the numbers from the cloud to complete this function machine.

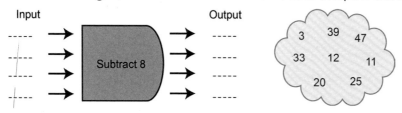

Input → Subtract 8 → Output
----- → → -----
----- → → -----
----- → → -----
----- → → -----

Cloud: 3   39   47   33   12   11   20   25

3 Write down two possible functions for each of these function machines.

a Input 4 → ? → Output 20

b Input 30 → ? → Output 5

4 Work out the outputs of these two-step function machines.

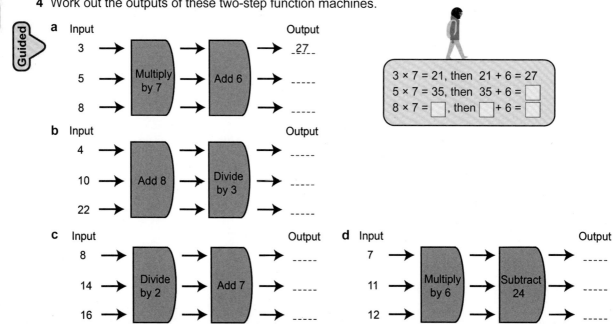

a Input → Multiply by 7 → Add 6 → Output
3 → → → 27
5 → → → -----
8 → → → -----

3 × 7 = 21, then 21 + 6 = 27
5 × 7 = 35, then 35 + 6 = ☐
8 × 7 = ☐, then ☐ + 6 = ☐

b Input → Add 8 → Divide by 3 → Output
4 → → → -----
10 → → → -----
22 → → → -----

c Input → Divide by 2 → Add 7 → Output
8 → → → -----
14 → → → -----
16 → → → -----

d Input → Multiply by 6 → Subtract 24 → Output
7 → → → -----
11 → → → -----
12 → → → -----

5 STEM   This function machine can be used to convert a temperature from degrees Celsius (°C) to degrees Fahrenheit (°F).

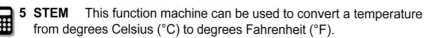

Temperature (°C) → Multiply by 1.8 → Add 32 → Temperature (°F)

Complete the table to show the temperatures in degrees Fahrenheit.

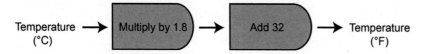

Temperature (°C)	0	14	22	30
Temperature (°F)				

6 In these brick pyramids, two adjacent bricks sum to give the brick above them. Write down the missing terms from these pyramids.

a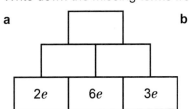

b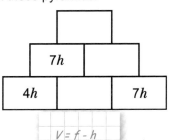

Literacy hint
A term is a number, a letter, or a number and a letter multiplied together.
expression
$$3x + 1$$
terms
'Adjacent' means beside or touching.

7 Suha uses the formula $V = f - h$.
This is what she writes.

$V = f - h$
$V = 20 - 11$
$= 9$

a Write down the value of f. ....

b Write down the value of h. ....

8 Here are two formulae. $A = 3b$ $D = A + C$

a Work out the value of A when $b = 8$.

Work out the value of A first.

b Work out the value of D when $A = 24$ and $C = 17$.

c Work out the value of D when $b = 5$ and $C = 28$.

9 Problem-solving Here are three formulae.
Work out the value of U when $q = 45$, $r = 7$ and $t = 9$.

$P = 18 + q$ $R = r \times t$ $U = P - R$

Decide which letters you need to find the values of before you can find U.

10 Maisie and Joe each have a bag of marbles.
Maisie's bag contains M marbles and Joe's bag contains J marbles.

a Write an expression for the total number of marbles in both bags.

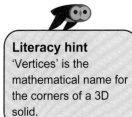

Maisie takes 5 marbles out of her bag and puts them in Joe's bag.

b i Write an expression for the number of marbles in Maisie's bag.

ii Write an expression for the number of marbles in Joe's bag.

11 STEM The number of edges on a 3D solid can be worked out by adding the number of faces and the number of vertices and then subtracting 2.

Literacy hint
'Vertices' is the mathematical name for the corners of a 3D solid.

a Work out the number of edges of a solid with

i 6 faces and 8 vertices

ii 5 faces and 6 vertices.

b Write a formula to work out the number of edges, E, when you know the number of faces, F, and the number of vertices, V.

Literacy hint
A dodecahedron is a solid shape made up of 12 regular pentagons.

c A dodecahedron has 12 faces and 20 vertices.
Work out how many edges it has.

33

PROGRESS BAR Colour in the progress bar as you get questions correct.
Then fill in the progression chart on pages 111–113.

1 Work out the outputs of these function machines.

a Input Output   **b** Input Output

7 → Add 10 → _____   15 → Subtract 6 → _____

c Input Output

3 → × 8 → _____

2 Write down the function for each machine.

a Input Output   **b** Input Output   **c** Input Output

3 → _____ → 18   4 → _____ → 24   15 → _____ → 5

5 → → 20   7 → → 42   19 → → 9

7 → → 22   9 → → 54   23 → → 13

3 Simplify

a $j + j + j$ _____   **b** $3k + 5k$ _____   **c** $3q + 4q + q$ _____

d $7f - 4f$ _____   **e** $9h - 7h$ _____   **f** $8d - d - 2d$ _____

4 Here are some algebra cards.
Choose two cards to make each statement correct.

$3d$ $10d$ $9d$ d $5d$ $7d$

i ⬚ + ⬚ = $14d$ **ii** ⬚ − ⬚ = $4d$

5 The formula to work out the number of cherry tomatoes needed for a recipe is
number of cherry tomatoes = 6 × number of people
Work out the number of cherry tomatoes needed for

a 4 people _____   **b** 10 people. _____

6 Sam earns £e per month.

a Aisha earns twice as much as Sam.
Write an expression for the amount Aisha earns per month. _____

b Ali earns £34 per month less than Sam.
Write an expression for the amount Ali earns per month. _____

7 $U = V + X$. Work out the value of U when $V = 25$ and $X = 14$.

8 $D = ST$. Work out the value of D when $S = 45$ and $T = 2$.

9 Riley is charged 10p for every minute of calls he makes on his phone.
Write a formula to work out the total cost, c, when you know the number of minutes, m.

1 Real The table shows the average temperatures in London for a week in March.

Day	Sat	Sun	Mon	Tue	Wed	Thu	Fri
Average temperature (°C)	12	10	11	9	10	11	14

Draw a graph to show these temperatures.

Put the temperatures on the vertical axis. Make sure you can fit on the highest and lowest temperatures.

Label the axes using the headings from the table.

Write a title for the graph – use words from the question.

Mark the points with crosses. Join them with straight lines.

For a graph showing how something changes over time, put time on the horizontal axis. For this graph, the time is in days.

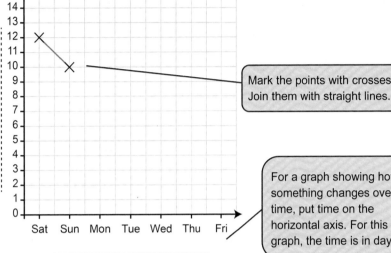

2 Real The graph shows the maximum temperatures in London for a week in August 2013.

a Look at the vertical axis. What values have been replaced by ⋛?

What values come before 16? What is the scale going up in?

b Which day was the hottest?

c What was the temperature on the hottest day?

d What days was the temperature 25 °C?

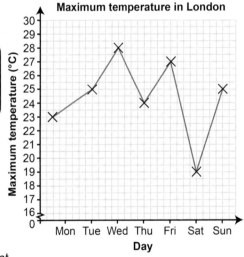

3 Real The graph shows the weight of a baby Asian elephant for the first 6 weeks.

a How much did the baby elephant weigh

Write kg with your answers.

  i at birth ....

  ii at 4 weeks? ....

b When did the baby elephant weigh 200 kg?

c How much weight did the baby elephant gain in

  i weeks 0–3 ....

  ii weeks 3–6? ....

CHECK Tick each box as your **confidence** in this topic improves.

Need extra help? Go to page 40 and tick the box next to Q7. Then have a go at it once you've finished 4.1–4.4.

4.2 Coordinates

1 Write down the coordinates of the points A, B, C and D.

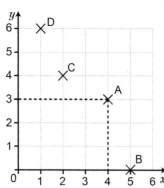

Start with point A. Move down to the x-axis to find the x-coordinate. Move across to the y-axis to find the y-coordinate.

The x-axis is the horizontal axis. The x-coordinate is the value on the x-axis. The y-axis is the vertical axis. The y-coordinate is the value on the y-axis. The x-coordinate and y-coordinate together tell you where a point is.

Write the coordinates in brackets like this: (x-coordinate, y-coordinate).

 Guided

A(4, ...), B(........, ...), C(........, ...), D(........, ...)

2 a Plot and label these points on the grid.

Mark each point carefully with a cross. Label it with its letter.

E(2, 1), F(6, 1), G(6, 5), H(2, 5)

b Join the points in order. Join the last point to the first. Use a ruler.

c What shape have you drawn? ....

d Draw in the diagonals of your shape.

e Write the coordinates of the point where they cross. ....

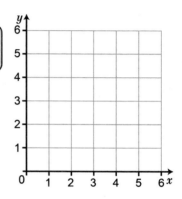

3 Write down the coordinates of the points J, K, L and M.

 Guided

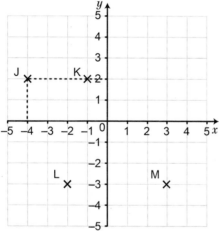

J(-4, ...)

K(........, ...)

L(........, ...)

M(........, ...)

Move up or down to the x-axis to find the x-coordinate. Move across to the y-axis to find the y-coordinate.

You can count back along the x-axis and the y-axis into negative values.

Worked example

4 Reasoning

a Plot and label these points on the grid.
A(3, 4), B(−2, 4), C(−2, −3)

b Join A and B, and B and C.
You have drawn two sides of a rectangle.

c Draw the other two sides.

d Write down the coordinates of the 4th vertex. ....

Literacy hint
Vertex means corner.

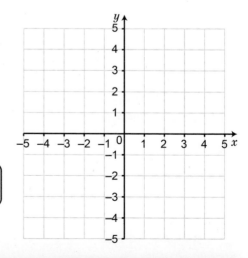

CHECK   Tick each box as your **confidence** in this topic improves.

Need extra help? Go to page 40 and tick the boxes next to Q1 and 2. Then have a go at them once you've finished 4.1–4.4.

36

1 a Complete the table of values for $y = x + 3$.

x	0	1	2	3
y	3			

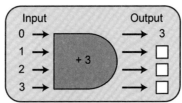

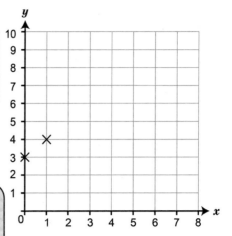

b Write down the coordinates from the table.

The coordinates are (0, 3), (......, ...),

(......, ...) and (......, ...).

c Plot your points and draw the graph. Label your line $y = x + 3$.

> Plot the points. Join them with a straight line to the edge of the grid.

2 Reasoning

a Complete this table of values for $y = 2x$.

x	0	1	2	3
y				

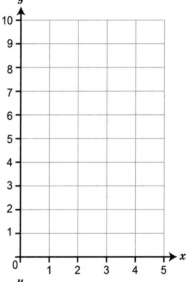

> Plot the points. Join them with a straight line to the edge of the grid. Label the line $y = 2x$.

b Draw the graph of $y = 2x$.

c Use your graph to work out

   i 4×2 ....

   ii 2.5×2 ....

   iii 0.5×2 ....

   iv 4.5×2 ....

3 Reasoning Complete this table of values from the graph.

x	0	1	2	3	4	5
y						

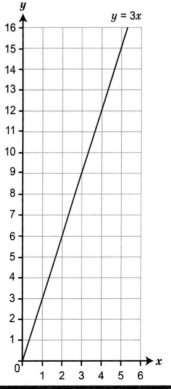

$y = 3x$

CHECK   Tick each box as your **confidence** in this topic improves.

Need extra help? Go to pages 40–41 and tick the boxes next to Q3–6. Then have a go at them once you've finished 4.1–4.4.

37

1 STEM Emma did an experiment with a rubber band. She hung different masses on the end of the rubber band and measured how much it extended.

a Draw a graph to show her results.

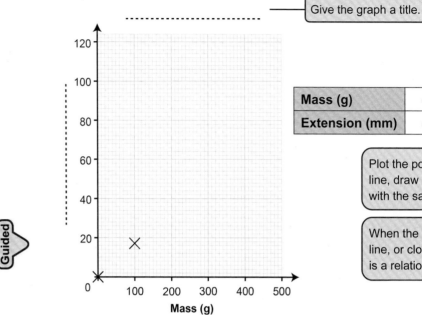

Give the graph a title.

Literacy hint
'Extended' means 'stretched'. The extension is how much the rubber band stretched.

Mass (g)	0	100	200	300	400
Extension (mm)	0	17	42	73	112

Plot the points. If they are close to a straight line, draw a straight line through the points, with the same number of points on each side.

When the points on a graph are on a straight line, or close to a straight line, it shows there is a relationship between the two values.

Mass (g)

 Guided

b Do you think there is a relationship between the amount of mass on the rubber band and the extension? If so, what is the relationship?

Some sets of data give a curved graph.

2 STEM / Reasoning Adam did an experiment to see if honey drips at different speeds at different temperatures. He heated the honey to different temperatures and timed how long it took to drip through a funnel.

a Draw a graph to show his results.

Temperature (°C)	Time to drip through (seconds)
30	86
35	55
40	21
45	12
50	10

b Join your points with a smooth curve.

c Use your graph to estimate the time taken for the honey to drip through at 32 °C.

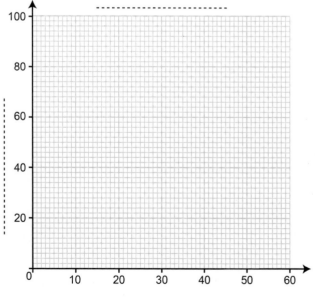

d Fill in the missing word.
As the temperature .... the honey gets runnier.

CHECK Tick each box as your **confidence** in this topic improves.

Need extra help? Go to page 40 and tick the box next to Q7. Then have a go at it once you've finished 4.1–4.4.

Coordinates

1 a Write down the *x*-coordinate for A. ....

> Put your finger on point A on the grid. Move your finger down to the *x*-axis.

b Write down the *y*-coordinate for A. ....

c Complete: A(........, ...)

> Put your finger on point A on the grid. Move your finger across to the *y*-axis.

> *x* comes before *y* in the alphabet.

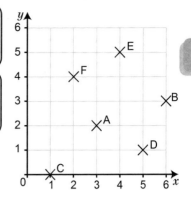

d Write down the coordinates of points B, C, D and E.

B(........, ...), C(........, ...), D(........, ...), E(........, ...)

e Freya says, 'The coordinates of F are (2, 3).' Is she correct? Explain.

> Write the coordinates of F. Compare them with Freya's.

2 a Write down the coordinates of the points P, Q, R, S, T, U, V and W.

P(........, ...)   Q(........, ...)

R(........, ...)   S(........, ...)

T(........, ...)   U(........, ...)

V(........, ...)   W(........, ...)

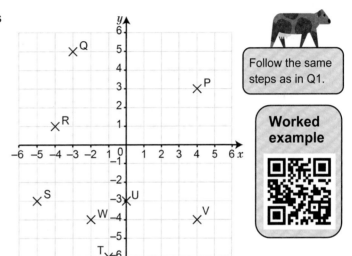

> Follow the same steps as in Q1.

> **Worked example**

b Plot and label these points on the grid.

A(2, 5)

B(−4, 4)

C(−3, −5)

Graphs of functions

3 Complete the function machine for

> What do you do to *x* to get *y*?

a $y = x + 7$ **b** $y = 3x$ **c** $y = x + 2$

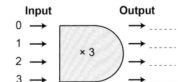

Input		Output
0 →		→ ......
1 →	+7	→ ......
2 →		→ ......
3 →		→ ......

Input		Output
0 →		→ ......
1 →	× 3	→ ......
2 →		→ ......
3 →		→ ......

Input		Output
0 →		→ ......
1 →	+ 2	→ ......
2 →		→ ......
3 →		→ ......

4 Complete the table of values for

> You could use your function machines from Q3 to help.

a $y = x + 7$ **b** $y = 3x$ **c** $y = x + 2$

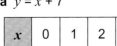
Guided

x	0	1	2	3
y	7			

x	0	1	2	3
y				

x	0	1	2	3
y				

> When *x* is 0, *y* is 0 + 7 = 7

5 Write down the coordinates to plot from each table of values you made in Q4.

Guided

a (0, 7), (1, ...), (2, ...), (3, ...)

b (0, ...), (1, ...), (2, ...), (3, ...)

c (........, ...), (........, ...), (........, ...), (........, ...)

(*x*-coordinate, *y*-coordinate)

6 Draw and label a graph for each table of values you made in Q4.

a
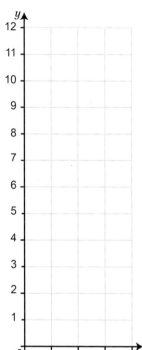

b
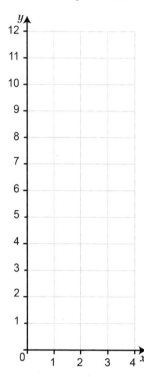

c

You could use your coordinates from Q5 to help.

Join the points with a straight line right to the edge of the grid.

Real-life and science graphs

7 Real The graph shows Roshni's temperature one afternoon.

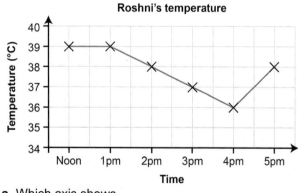

a Which axis shows

  i the temperature ....

  ii the time? ....

b What was the first temperature reading? ....

c What was Roshni's temperature at 2 pm? ....

d When was Roshni's temperature 37 °C? ....

e When was her minimum (lowest) temperature? ....

Strategy hint
Before you start a graph question, read the title and the labels on the axes to see what they show.

Worked example

Find 2 pm on the Time axis. Move your finger up to the graph line. Now move your finger straight across to the Temperature axis.

Start at 37 on the Temperature axis. Go across to the graph line and down to the Time axis.

1 Reasoning / Problem-solving

a Plot these points on the grid.

(−4, 3), (3, 3), (3, −2)

b These points are all corners of a rectangle.
Write down the coordinates of the 4th corner.

> Draw in the sides of the rectangle to help you see where the 4th corner will be.

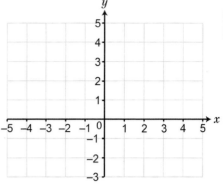

2 Reasoning / Problem-solving

a Complete this table of values from the graph.

x	0	1	2	3	4	5
y						

b Fill in the missing number.
The y-values go up by .... each time.

c Which times tables does the graph show? Explain.

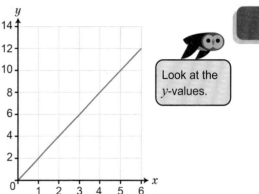

> Look at the y-values.

d Write four multiplication and division questions you could answer using this graph.

3 Here is a table of values for $y = 3$.
For every x-value, the y-value is 3.

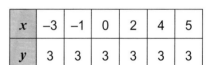

x	−3	−1	0	2	4	5
y	3	3	3	3	3	3

a Plot the points from the table on the grid.
Join them with a straight line. Label your line $y = 3$.

b Complete a table of values for $y = 1$.

x						
y						

c Plot your points on the grid.
Join them with a straight line. Label your line $y = 1$.

d Reasoning Draw and label the line $y = -2$ on the grid.

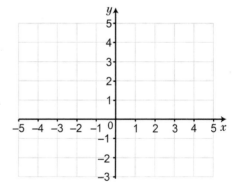

4 Here is a table of values for $x = 2$.
For every y-value, the x-value is 2.

x	2	2	2	2	2	2
y	−3	−1	0	1	2	3

a Plot the points from the table on the grid.
Join them with a straight line. Label your line $x = 2$.

b Reasoning Draw and label the line $x = 3$ on the grid.

c Reasoning Draw and label the line $x = -2$ on the grid.

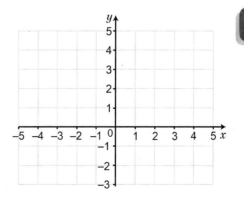

5 Reasoning / Real To create a CGI movie, programmers have to explain to the computer what to draw, and where. Label the lines on each diagram the computer needs to draw to make

a this rectangle

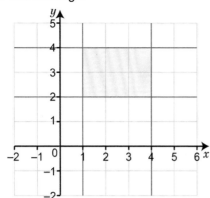

b this square.

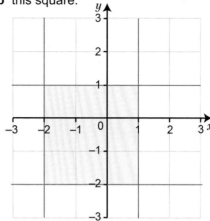

6 Real / Problem-solving The graph shows the costs for printing photographs. You upload your photographs online and then can either have them posted to your home or collect from your local store.

a Callum wants 50 photographs printed. Which service should he use? Explain.

b Hollie wants 20 photographs printed. Which service should she use? Explain.

c How much is the home delivery charge?

d Complete the sentence with the correct number. The 'post to home' service is better value if you want more than .... photographs printed.

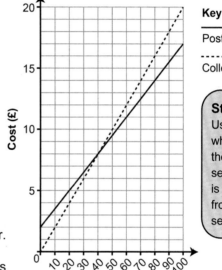

Key

—— Post to home

------ Collect from store

Strategy hint
Use the key to see which line is for the 'post to home' service and which is for the 'collect from store' service.

7 Real / Problem-solving The graph shows the average rainfall and maximum temperature each month in Florida.

a Which is the wettest month in Florida?

b Which months are the hottest in Florida?

c Work out the range of the temperatures and the range of the rainfall in Florida.

d Jane and her family are travelling to Florida for a holiday in April. Write a sentence to tell her what the weather should be like.

Florida maximum temperatures and average rainfall

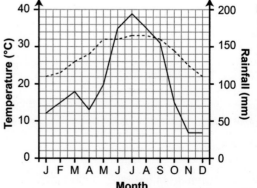

Key

—— Rainfall

------ Temperature

Strategy hint
Use the key to see which line is for rainfall and which line is for temperature. Read the vertical axes to see which is for temperature and which is for rainfall.

4 Unit test

> **PROGRESS BAR** Colour in the progress bar as you get questions correct. Then fill in the progression chart on pages 111–113.

1 Write down the coordinates of the points marked with letters.

A(....... , ...)   B(....... , ...)

C(....... , ...)   D(....... , ...)

E(....... , ...)   F(....... , ...)

G(....... , ...)   H(....... , ...)

J(....... , ...)   K(....... , ...)

L(....... , ...)   M(....... , ...)

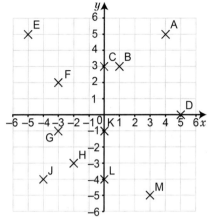

2 a Complete the table of values for the function $y = x + 4$.

x	0	1	2	3
y				

b Draw the graph of $y = x + 4$. Label your line $y = x + 4$.

c Use the graph to find the value of

    i y when $x = 1\frac{1}{2}$ ....

    ii x when $y = 8\frac{1}{2}$ ....

3 The graph shows Josh and Claire's savings.

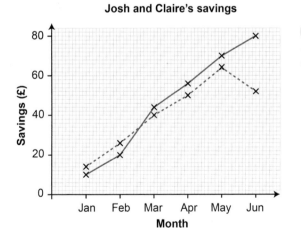

Josh and Claire's savings

Key
..... Josh
— Claire

a When does Josh have £64? ....

b How much money does Claire have in June? ....

c How much does Josh save from January to February? ....

d Who has more money in February? ....

e Who has more money in June? ....

f Who spends some of their savings? Explain how you know.

1 Work out

a 5 + 3 × 4 ——————

> Work out the multiplication first.

> The operation keys on a calculator are +, −, × and ÷. To get the answer, press the '=' key.

= 5 + ... = ...

b 12 ÷ 4 − 1 ....

c 5 + 6 ÷ 2 ....

d 18 − 5 × 2 ....

> Multiplication and Division *before* Addition and Subtraction.

e 15 − 12 ÷ 3 ....

f 7 × 3 − 8 ....

g 35 ÷ 5 + 6 ....

2 Circle the calculations that have the same answer.

3 × 4 + 5 × 2   7 + 5 × 3   6 × 5 − 2 × 4   20 − 2 × 3   20 ÷ 5 + 6 × 3

3 Work out

a 2 × 6 × 5 ....

b 4 × 30 × 7 ....

c 3 × 8 × 4 × 5 ....

> Multiplication can be done in any order.

4 Reasoning Work out each pair of calculations.

a i 7 + 8 ....

b i 78 + 53 ....

c i 9 − 5 ....

d i 57 − 39 ....

ii 8 + 7 ....

ii 53 + 78 ....

ii 5 − 9 ....

ii 39 − 57 ....

e i Which pairs of calculations have the same answer as each other? ....

ii Which pairs of calculations don't have the same answer? ....

iii Use the words *addition* or *subtraction* to complete these sentences:

'............ can be done in any order.'

'The order is important in ....'

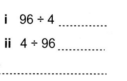

> The '−' sign before an answer on the calculator means that the answer is a negative number.

5 Reasoning Use a calculator to work out each pair of calculations.

a i 3 × 8 ....

b i 23 × 16 ....

c i 50 ÷ 5 ....

d i 96 ÷ 4 ....

ii 8 × 3 ....

ii 16 × 23 ....

ii 5 ÷ 50 ....

ii 4 ÷ 96 ....

e i Which pairs of calculations have the same answer as each other? ....

ii Which pairs of calculations don't have the same answer? ....

iii Use the words *multiplication* or *division* to complete these sentences:

'............ can be done in any order.'

'The order is important in ....'

6 Work these out, from left to right.

a 4 × 9 ÷ 12 ....

b 24 ÷ 6 × 11 ....

c 42 ÷ 2 ÷ 7 ....

> When you have only × and ÷, or only + and −, then just work from left to right.

d 16 + 35 + 14 ....

e 18 + 23 − 26 ....

f 46 − 19 − 12 ....

CHECK   Tick each box as your **confidence** in this topic improves.

Need extra help? Go to page 51 and tick the box next to Q1. Then have a go at it once you've finished 5.1–5.7.

5.2 Multiples

1 a Write the first 10 multiples of 2.

b Complete the sentence:
'Multiples of 2 are all _____ numbers.'

c Write each number in the correct
column in the table.

367	632	999	1001
3754	4223	7268	11 970

Odd	Even

> A multiple of a number
> is in that number's
> multiplication table.

> The last digit of an odd
> number is 1, 3, 5, 7 or 9.
> The last digit of an even
> number is 2, 4, 6, 8 or 0.

2 a Write the first 10 multiples of 10.

b Circle the multiples of 10.   20   26   30   40   45   60

3 a Write the first 10 multiples of 5.

b Circle the multiples of 5.   40   45   48   50   53   55

4 True or false?

> Look back at the multiples you
> wrote in Q1, Q2 and Q3.

a 46 is a multiple of 2 _____   **b** 18 is a multiple of 5 _____

c 23 is a multiple of 10 _____   **d** 45 is a multiple of 5 _____

e 40 is a multiple of 10 _____   **f** 35 is a multiple of 2 _____

5 a Write the first 10 multiples of 3.

b Circle the multiples of 3.   21   22   24   26   27   29

6 a Write the first 10 multiples of 25.

25, 50, 75,

b What pattern do you notice in your list of multiples? _____

c Circle the multiples of 25.   340   575   825   920   980

7 Reasoning   Choose a number to make these statements true.

a 18 is a multiple of _____

> The last digit of 18 is 8, so 18 is an
> even number.
> All even numbers are multiples of 2.

b 20 is a multiple of _____   **c** 35 is a multiple of _____

8 Reasoning   Circle the odd one out in each of these lists.
Explain your reason using the word 'multiple'.

> **Strategy hint**
> Are they multiples
> of 2? Or 3?

a 6, 14, 23, 32, 44 _____

b 20, 50, 60, 77, 80 _____

c 6, 10, 12, 15, 21 _____

CHECK   Tick each box as your **confidence** in this topic improves.

Need extra help? Go to page 53 and tick the box next to Q21. Then have a go at it once you've finished 5.1–5.7.

1 Match each number to its nearest 100.

751 578 610 845 733

600 —— 700 —— 800

For rounding to the nearest 100
• 50 and above rounds up
• 49 and below rounds down.

rounds down   rounds up

200   250   300

2 Round each number to the nearest 1000.

a 6500 ....   **b** 4470 ....

c 1099 ....   **d** 23 457 ....

For rounding to the nearest 1000
• 500 and above rounds up
• 499 and below rounds down.

rounds down   rounds up

7000   7500   8000

3 a Estimate each multiplication below by rounding to the nearest 100.

b Work out the exact answer to each multiplication.
Use your estimate to check that your answer looks sensible.

Estimation means making a good guess.
Using rounding is a good way to estimate because it helps to check that your answer is sensible.

i 398 × 4

'≈' means 'approximately equal to'.

Estimate: 398 × 4 ≈ 400 × 4 = ...

×	300	90	8
4	1200		

1200 + ... + ...

Split the larger number into hundreds, tens and units.
Write them along the top of a grid.
Write 4 at the side of the grid.
Multiply each part separately and write the answer in each space.

Add the three parts together.

+ ——
——

Check: .... is reasonably close to ....

Check your answer against the estimate.

ii 207 × 6

Estimate:

×			

Check:

iii 8 × 592

Estimate:

×			

Check:

4 Finance A flight from the UK to Florida costs £728.
How much would this flight cost for 6 people?

Use the column method.

728
×   6
————
    8
  4

Multiply each digit in the top row by the digit in the bottom row.
Start in the units column: 6 × 8 = 48
That's 4 tens and 8 units.

728
×   6
————
  68
 1 4

In the tens column: 6 × 2 = 12
                12 + 4 = 16
That's 16 tens altogether.

In the hundreds column: 6 × 7 = 42
                  42 + 1 = 43

5 A book has 347 pages.
How many pages are there in 8 books?

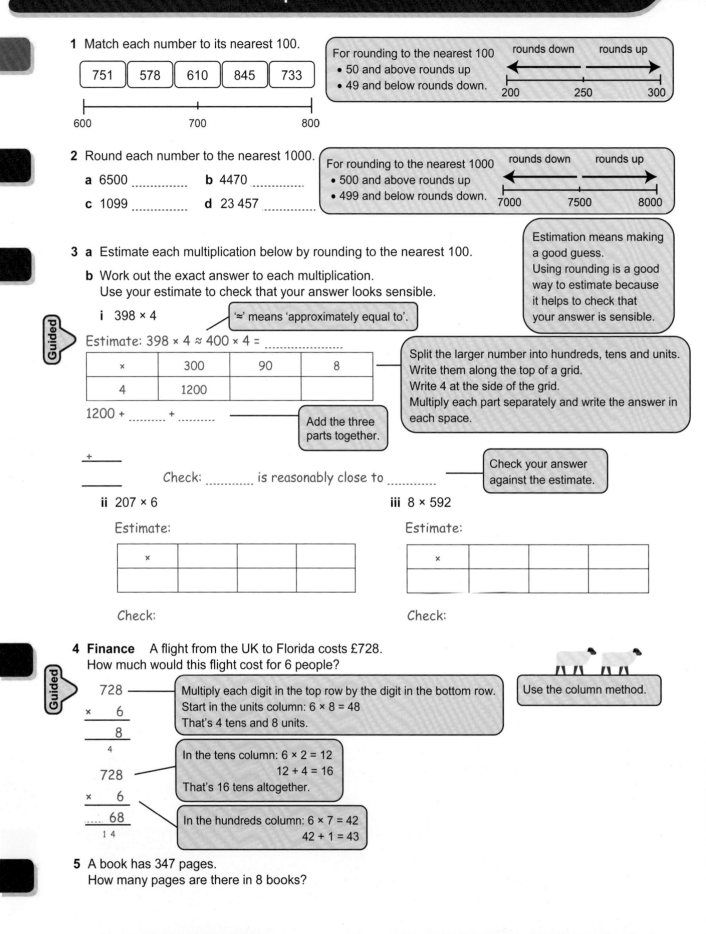

CHECK   Tick each box as your **confidence** in this topic improves.

Need extra help? Go to page 51 and tick the boxes next to Q2–7. Then have a go at them once you've finished 5.1–5.7.

5.4 Division

1 Complete these.

   a 4 × 10 = 40, 40 ÷ 10 = ...   **b** 9 × 10 = 90, 90 ÷ 10 = ...

   c A multiple of 10 divides by ....

2 Circle the numbers that divide by 10.   20   34   46   50   55   60

> Are they in the 10 times table?

3 Complete these.

   a 3 × 5 = 15, 15 ÷ 5 = ...   **b** 8 × 5 = 40, 40 ÷ 5 = ...

   c A multiple of 5 divides by ....

4 Circle the numbers that divide by 5.   20   34   46   50   55   60

5 Complete these sentences.

   a The last digit of a multiple of 10 is ....

   b The last digit of a multiple of 5 is .... or ....

   c All multiples of 2 are .... numbers.

6 a Write the first 12 multiples of 9.

   b Circle the numbers that divide by 9.   261   344   460   504   621   850

> Numbers are divisible by 9 if the digits total 9. e.g. 63 is a multiple of 9 and 6 + 3 = 9.

7 Use the bar models to work out these.

   a 234 ÷ 6   234 ÷ 6   =   (180 ÷ 6) + (54 ÷ 6)

                                      30   +   ☐

   234 ÷ 6 = 30 + ☐ = ☐

   b 165 ÷ 5   165 ÷ 5   =   (100 ÷ 5) + (50 ÷ 5) + (15 ÷ 5)

                                   ☐   +   ☐   +   ☐

   165 ÷ 5 = ☐ + ☐ + ☐ = ☐

8 Use a written method to work out these divisions.

   a 917 ÷ 7

             1
      7 | 9 ²1 7

> Look at the digits in 917, starting on the left.
> 7 goes into 9 once, so write a 1 in the hundreds column above.
> The difference between 9 and 7 is 2, so write these 2 hundreds in the tens column, to make 21 tens.

          1 3 ......
      7 | 9 ²1 7

> 7 goes into 21 exactly 3 times, so write a 3 in the tens column above.

> 7 goes into 7 exactly once, so write a 1 in the units column above.

   b 845 ÷ 5 ....   **c** 536 ÷ 8 ....   **d** 477 ÷ 9 ....   **e** 942 ÷ 6 ....

CHECK   Tick each box as your **confidence** in this topic improves.   😞 😐 😊

Need extra help? Go to page 52 and tick the boxes next to Q8–11. Then have a go at them once you've finished 5.1–5.7.

5.5 Solving problems

1 Real A people carrier can take 7 people.
How many people carriers would 189 people need?

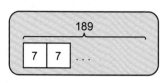

2 Real Ali earns £9 per hour.
How much does she earn for 4 hours' work?

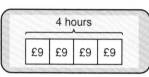

3 It is 161 days until Pete goes on holiday. How many weeks is it until Pete goes on holiday?

4 What is the total cost of 6 books that are £3.49 each?

> Convert the price into pence to make a 3-digit number.

5 Real Eggs are packed in trays of 15.
How many trays would you need to pack 285 eggs?

6 Apples are sold in bags of 8. How many apples are there in 27 bags?

7 Real / Problem-solving Circle the correct calculation for each problem. Then work it out.

a Farmer Hine's 32 chickens each lay 6 eggs every week.
How many 12-egg trays per week will he need to pack them?

$$32 \times 6 \times 12 \qquad 32 \times 6 \div 12 \qquad 32 + 6 - 12 \qquad 32 \times 6 - 12$$

> Multiplication and Division *before* Addition and Subtraction.

b Chocolate bars from the wholesaler are sold in boxes of 48 trays, with 8 bars on each tray.
Josh buys 6 boxes. How many chocolate bars is that?

$$8 \times 48 + 6 \qquad 8 \times 48 \div 8 \qquad 8 \times 48 \times 6 \qquad 8 + 48 \times 6$$

 8 How many minibuses carrying 16 people each are needed to take 100 students on a school trip?

> There needs to be a space for everyone, so does the answer need to round up or down?

CHECK Tick each box as your **confidence** in this topic improves.

Need extra help? Go to page 52 and tick the boxes next to Q12–15. Then have a go at them once you've finished 5.1–5.7.

5.6 Factors and primes

1 Follow these steps to find all the factors of 20.

a Is 1 a factor? $1 \times \underline{\quad} = 20$ ── So 1 and ☐ are a factor pair.

b Is 2 a factor? $2 \times \underline{\quad} = 20$ ── So 2 and ☐ are a factor pair.

c Is 3 a factor? $3 \times \underline{\quad} = 20$

So 3 is *not* a factor of 20.

d Is 4 a factor? $4 \times \underline{\quad} = 20$

So 4 and ☐ are a factor pair.

e Is 5 a factor? ....

f Have you found all the factors of 20? ....

g List all the factors of 20. ....

> A factor is a whole number that will divide exactly into another number.
> A factor pair is two numbers that multiply together to make a number.

> List all the factors you have found in order, smallest first.

2 a Complete each of these diagrams to show the factor pairs of the number in the middle.

i **ii** **iii** **iv**

b Write the factors in a list.

i The factors of 8 are: 1, ..., ..., ...

ii The factors of 22 are: 1, ..., ..., ...

iii The factors of 35 are: 1, ..., ..., ...

iv The factors of 12 are: 1, ..., ..., ..., ..., ...

> The opposite numbers multiply together to make the middle number.
> So the opposite numbers are a factor pair of the middle number.

3 Write all the factors of

a 9 ....

b 24 ....

c 34 ....

Put them into factor pairs to check that you've got them all.

> Where there is a repeated factor (for example, 5 × 5), just write it once in the list of factors.

4 Write all the factors of

a 2 ....

b 7 ....

c 13 ....

d What do you notice about your answers?

> A prime number has exactly two different factors: 1 and itself.
> 1 is not a prime number because it only has one factor.

5 Reasoning Circle the prime numbers.

5   10   11   15   19   20   23   25   27

> Does the number have exactly two factors, or more than two?

6 Reasoning Write a number to fit each description.

a A multiple of 2 that is also a factor of 32 ....

b A factor of both 12 and 20 ....

c A prime number between 20 and 30 ....

d A multiple of both 3 and 4 ....

CHECK Tick each box as your **confidence** in this topic improves.

Need extra help? Go to page 53 and tick the boxes next to Q16–20 and 22. Then have a go at them once you've finished 5.1–5.7.

5.7 Common factors and multiples

1 Circle the multiples of 4.

20   50   68   90   112   300   314   512

> • Half of a multiple of 4 is an even number.
> • If you halve a multiple of 4, then halve it again, you get a whole number.

2 Problem-solving Use these number cards to make a 2-digit number and a 3-digit number to match each statement.

2 3 4 5 6 7 8 9

a 4 is a factor of ☐☐ and ☐☐☐

b 3 is a factor of ☐☐ and ☐☐☐

c ☐☐ and ☐☐☐ are multiples of 5

d ☐☐ and ☐☐☐ are multiples of 9

> **Tests of divisibility**
> • Divisible by 3 if the digits add to a multiple of 3
> • Divisible by 6 if it is even *and* divisible by 3
> • Divisible by 9 if the digits add to a multiple of 9

3 Work out the HCF of each pair of numbers.

a 18 and 30

Guided

Factors of 18: ①, ②, ③, ..., ..., ...

Factors of 30: ①, ②, ③, ..., ..., ..., ..., ...

Common factors: 1, 2, 3, ...

HCF: .... —— Find the *largest* number in the list of common factors.

> **Worked example**

> A common factor of two numbers is a factor of both numbers.
> The highest common factor (HCF) of two numbers is the *largest* number that is a factor of both numbers.

> Write lists of factors of both numbers. Circle the factors that appear in both lists.

b 21 and 35   **c** 24 and 40

4 Work out the LCM of each pair of numbers.

a 6 and 8

Guided

Multiples of 6: 6, 12, 18, ㉔ 30, 36, 42, ㊽

Multiples of 8: 8, 16, ㉔ 32, 40, ㊽ 56, 64

LCM: ....

> Write lists of multiples of both numbers. Circle the multiples that appear in both lists.

> Find the *smallest* number that is in both lists.

> A common multiple of two numbers is a multiple of both numbers.
> The lowest common multiple (LCM) of two numbers is the *smallest* number that is a multiple of both numbers.

b 4 and 7   **c** 6 and 10

5 A pack of burgers holds 4 burgers. Burger buns come in packs of 6.

a What is the LCM of 4 and 6?

b How many packs of burgers and packs of buns do you need to buy to make sure no burgers and no buns are left over?

CHECK   Tick each box as your **confidence** in this topic improves.

Need extra help? Go to page 53 and tick the box next to Q21. Then have a go at it once you've finished 5.1–5.7.

Multiplication and number rules

1 Use the correct priority of operations to work out these calculations. Put brackets round the part that needs to be worked out first.

> Multiplication and Division *before* Addition and Subtraction.

a $4 + 3 \times 2 = 4 + (3 \times 2) = 4 +$ .... = ...

b $40 \div 5 + 3$ ....

c $20 - 21 \div 3$ ....

d $4 \times 6 - 8$ ....

2 Complete this table for the 12 times table.

×	1	2	5	10	20	50	100
12							

3 Use the table from Q2 to work out

a 30×12

×	12
10	120
20	240
30	

b 155×12

×	12
5	
50	
100	
155	

c 161×12

×	12

d 205×12

×	12

4 Use the grids to work out these multiplications.

a $263 \times 7 =$

×	7
200	
60	
3	
263	

b $138 \times 6 =$

×	6
100	
30	
8	
138	

c $439 \times 8 =$

×	8
400	
30	
9	
439	

5 Use rounding to estimate the answer to

a 63×8 ....

b 4×48 ....

c 77×9 ....

d 5×55 ....

> 63 is approximately ☐
> And ☐ × 8 = ☐

6 Use rounding to estimate the answer to

a 188×3 ....

b 5×106 ....

c 167×4 ....

d 3×289 ....

> Round 188 to the nearest 100.

7 Use the grids to work out these multiplications.

a 27×32 ....

×	**20**	**7**
30	30 × 20 =	30 × 7 =
2	..... × ..... =	..... × ..... =

b 16×43 ....

×	**10**	**6**
40		
3		

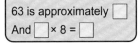

Worked example

Work out the missing answers in the grid and then add them together.

51

Division

8 Write each division answer with a remainder.

a $10 \div 3 = 3$ remainder 1

b $17 \div 5 =$ .... remainder ....

c $40 \div 9 =$ .... remainder ....

d $18 \div 4 =$ .... remainder ....

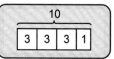

9 Work out

a $3\overline{)9}$ ....

b $4\overline{)48}$ ....

c $2\overline{)684}$ ....

d $3\overline{)936}$ ....

10 Work out

a $3\overline{)27}$ ....

> 3 doesn't go into 2, so work out how many 3s go into 27.

b $5\overline{)435}$ ....

c $4\overline{)592}$ ....

d $6\overline{)534}$ ....

e $676 \div 4$ ....

11 Work out

a $4\overline{)5\,^13}$ with quotient 1 ....

> How many 4s go into 5?
> What's the remainder?
> $1\,\square\ r\,\square$
> $4\overline{)5\,^13}$

b $3\overline{)253}$ ....

c $5\overline{)432}$ ....

d $6\overline{)215}$ ....

e $532 \div 9$ ....

Solving problems

12 **Problem-solving** A school has 196 students and 7 equal size classes. How many are in each class?

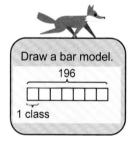

Draw a bar model.
196
1 class

13 **Problem-solving** A camping trip to France costs £283 per person. What is the total cost for 4 people?

14 **Reasoning** Sophie answers the question, 'How many 10-seater minibuses do you need for 34 people?', like this:

$34 \div 10 = 3$ remainder 4

So you need 3 minibuses.

Is she right? Explain your answer.

> Will all 34 people fit in 3 minibuses?

15 **Problem-solving** How many 5 m*l* doses of medicine are in a 275 m*l* bottle?

52

Multiples, factors and primes

16 Complete these labels. The first one has been started for you.

a 3 × 5 = 15

factor of 15	.... of 15	multiple of 3 .... of 5

b 2 × 6 = 12

.... of 12	.... of 12	.... of 2 .... of 6

17 Write down

a two factors of 10 ....

b two factors of 16 ....

c two multiples of 6 ....

Write a multiplication first.
☐ × ☐ = 10

18 Find the factors of

a 9

1 × .... = 9

3 × .... = 9

Factors of 9 are 1, 3, ...

b 30

c 24

d 50

19 a Circle the numbers with 2 as a factor.　　6　　18　　23　　31　　207　　348

　　b Circle the numbers with 10 as a factor.　　10　　15　　30　　460　　575　　940

　　c Circle the numbers with 5 as a factor.　　6　　15　　20　　30　　205　　345

20 Complete this sentence about prime numbers, using the correct number in each space.

'A prime number has only .... factors: .... and itself.'

21 Use these sets of multiples to help you.

First 10 multiples of 4

8	16	28	32	36
20	4	12	24	40

First 10 multiples of 5

45	40	35	5	50
25	30	10	20	15

First 10 multiples of 6

54	42	18	12	6
36	24	30	60	48

This Venn diagram shows the common multiples of 4 and 5.

Complete the Venn diagrams to show the common multiples of

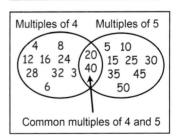
Multiples of 4　　Multiples of 5
4　8
12　16　24　20
28　32　3　40　15　25　30
6　　35　45　50
Common multiples of 4 and 5

a 4 and 6

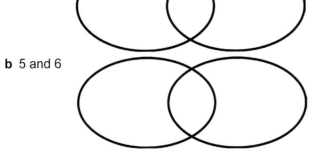

b 5 and 6

22 Circle the prime numbers.

　　3　　7　　9　　11　　13　　15　　23

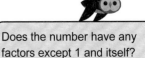
Does the number have any factors except 1 and itself?

1 Work out

a 3 × 4 × 5 × 2 ....   **b** 4 × 9 × 5 ....   **c** 6 × 8 − 56 ÷ 7 ....   *Use the priority of operations.*

d 32 ÷ 4 + 3 × 7 ....   **e** 20 − 30 ÷ 5 − 4 ....   **f** 12 + 4 × 7 − 13 ....

2 Reasoning Use the fact that 15 × 38 = 570 to work out

a 570 ÷ 38 = ...   **b** 570 ÷ 19 = ...   **c** 30 × 38 = ...

d 15 × 76 = ...   **e** 19 × 15 = ...   **f** 570 ÷ 76 = ...

Strategy hint
Look for doubles and halves of the calculation you have been given.

3 Use a written method to multiply

a 3157 × 4   **b** 1382 × 9   **c** 2064 × 7

Worked example

Use the same method for 4-digit numbers as you used for 3-digit numbers.

4 Work out

a 4765 ÷ 5   **b** 3576 ÷ 4   **c** 7431 ÷ 3   **d** 3174 ÷ 6

5 Reasoning All of these divisions have a remainder. For each one, explain how you can tell.

a 867 ÷ 4 ....

b 413 ÷ 3 ....

c 747 ÷ 5 ....

6 Problem-solving What different size teams could a group of 45 students be arranged in, without anyone being left out?

 Guided

1 team of 45, 3 teams of ....

Use factor pairs.

7 Reasoning Lauren works in a supermarket. She wants to arrange 36 tins in equal rows. How could she arrange them?

8 Problem-solving 93 musicians want to enter a battle of the bands competition.

a How many bands of 5 can they make? How many musicians are left over?

b There must be one teacher for every 12 musicians. How many teachers do they need?

c The teams will travel to the competition in minibuses. Each minibus can carry 16 passengers. How many minibuses will they need?

Passengers include teachers and musicians.

9 Choose the missing word for each sentence.

divisible   even   factors   multiples   odd   prime   square   factor

a 25 is not prime because it has more than two _____ .

b No even numbers greater than 2 are prime because they are _____ of 2.

c All _____ numbers have only two factors.

d 33 is not prime because it is _____ by 3 and by 11.

e 1 is not prime because it has only one _____ .

10 Real   Pencils come in boxes of 144. A school buys 12 boxes. How many pencils is this altogether?

11 Real / Finance

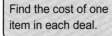

Find the cost of one item in each deal.

a Which is better value, £6.30 for a pack of 42 fun-size chocolate bars or £7.20 for a pack of 45 fun-size chocolate bars?

b Which is better value, 8 batteries for £5.50 or 20 batteries for £12?

Worked example

12 Reasoning   True or false? Write one or two calculations to explain each answer.

a 24 is a square number. _____

b 630 is a multiple of 9. _____

c 42 is a factor of 7. _____

d 81 is a square number. _____

e A number can be both a factor and a multiple of a number. _____

13 a Write each number in the correct place on the Venn diagram.

Guided

12   2   4   13

3   5   11   14

7   8   10   15

9   6   1   16

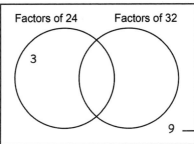

Factors of 24   Factors of 32

3

9

Where do you put a number that is a factor of both 24 and 32?

A number that is *not* a factor of either 24 or 32 goes *outside* the circles but *inside* the rectangle.

b What are the common factors of 24 and 32? _____

c What is the highest common factor of 24 and 32? _____

14 Draw Venn diagrams to find the common factors and the highest common factor of each pair of numbers.

a 36 and 45   **b** 24 and 40

5 Unit test

PROGRESS BAR Colour in the progress bar as you get questions correct. Then fill in the progression chart on pages 111–113.

1 Circle the multiples of 3.

15   20   39   63   73   200   201

2 Work out

a 485 ÷ 5 _____   **b** 368 × 4 _____   **c** 432 ÷ 6 _____   **d** 251 × 8 _____

3 a Divide 35 by

i 3 _____   **ii** 4 _____   **iii** 9 _____

b Which has the largest remainder? _____

4 Work out

a 4 + 3 × 6 − 5 _____   **b** 30 ÷ 6 × 5 _____   **c** 40 ÷ 8 − 5 + 9 _____

5 Write down all the factors of

a 14 _____   **b** 18 _____   **c** 30 _____

6 What is the highest common factor of 24 and 30?

7 What is the lowest common multiple of 5 and 8?

8 Circle the prime numbers.

31   33   35   37   39

9 Write whether each statement is true or false.

a 64 is a square number. _____

b 251 is a multiple of 9. _____

c 8 is a factor of 32. _____

d 32 is a factor of 8. _____

e 41 is a prime number. _____

10 Charm bracelets are made using 8 charms.
How many bracelets can be made with 270 charms?

1 Reasoning Circle the unit you would use to measure each item.

   a the height of a lamppost   m   litres   g

   b the mass of a suitcase   cm   litres   kg

   c the capacity of an eggcup   cm   m*l*   g

> Height measures how tall an object is.
> Mass measures how much something weighs.
> Capacity is the amount or volume that a container can hold.

2 Write the measurement shown by each arrow.

> What is each small space on the scale? Write the units with your answer.

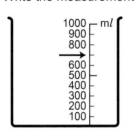

a ....   **b i** ....   **c i** ....

                                  ii ....   **ii** ....

3 Estimate the measurements shown on these scales.

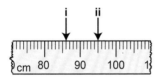

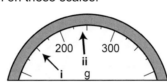

Strategy hint
Is the arrow halfway between two values? Is it closer to one value?

a i ....   **b i** ....

  ii ....   **ii** ....

4 Draw lines of length

   a 5 cm

   b 8 cm

   c 14 cm

Worked example

5 For each line **i** estimate its length   **ii** measure it accurately.

   a ——————   **i** ....   **ii** ....

   b ————————————   **i** ....   **ii** ....

   c ————————————————— **i** ....   **ii** ....

6 Reasoning Circle the most suitable unit of length to measure each item.

   a the width of this book   mm   cm   m   km

   b the distance between two cities   mm   cm   m   km

   c the length of your bed   mm   cm   m   km

   d the thickness of this book   mm   cm   m   km

CHECK Tick each box as your **confidence** in this topic improves.

Need extra help? Go to page 65 and tick the box next to Q12. Then have a go at it once you've finished 6.1–6.7.

57

6.2 Decimal numbers

1 Write the decimal number shown in each diagram.

a

b

c

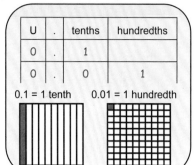

U	.	tenths	hundredths
0	.	1	
0	.	0	1

0.1 = 1 tenth   0.01 = 1 hundredth

U	.	tenths
0	.	7

U	.	tenths	hundredths
0	.	0	4

0.7   ....

2 Write the measurement in cm shown by each arrow. Give each measurement to 1 decimal place.

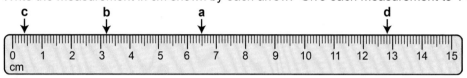

a ....   **b** ....   **c** ....   **d** ....

3 Draw lines of length

a 6.3 cm

b 4.8 cm

There are ten 1 mm spaces in 1 cm.
1 mm space is one tenth
of 1 cm = 0.1 cm

6 cm   3 spaces = 0.3 cm

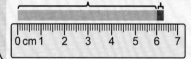

4 There are 10 tenths in 1. How many tenths are in

a 3.5 ....   **b** 10.2 ....

c 15.9 ....   **d** 31.6? ....

5 What is the value of the 7 in each of these numbers?

a 4.70 ....   **b** 10.67 ....   **c** 57.29 ....   **d** 9.07 ....

6 Write the measurement shown by each arrow.

a ....   **b** ....

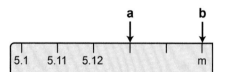

5.1   5.11   5.12   m

7 Complete these heights.

a 1 m 53 cm = 1.53 m   **b** 1 m 24 cm = 1. .... m

c 1 m 60 cm = ... m   **d** 1 m 6 cm = ... m

e 2 m 4 cm = ... m   **f** 1 m 90 cm = ... m

8 Write < or > between each pair of numbers.

a 5.4 .... 5.7   **b** 3.5 .... 3.1   **c** 7.06 .... 7.02

d 9.09 .... 9.1   **e** 6.5 .... 6.52   **f** 6.88 .... 6.9

1 First compare the whole number parts.
2 If these are the same, compare the tenths.
3 If these are also the same, compare the hundredths.

9 Write these decimal numbers in order, from smallest to largest.

a 3.21   3.16   3.28   3.19   3.25 ....

b 5.4   5.31   5.6   5.55   5.3 ....

CHECK Tick each box as your **confidence** in this topic improves.

Need extra help? Go to pages 64–5 and tick the boxes next to Q1–4 and 13. Then have a go at them once you've finished 6.1–6.7.

6.3 Metric units

1 a Write the measurement shown by each arrow in cm and in mm.

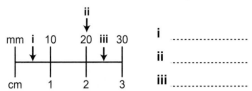

i ....

ii ....

iii ....

> 1 centimetre (cm) = 10 millimetres (mm)

b How many mm is 4 cm? ....

c How many cm is 70 mm? ....

2 Write these lengths in order, smallest first.

> Convert them all to the same units.

a 45 mm   4 cm   60 mm   5.5 cm ....

b 130 mm   10.6 cm   103 cm   103 mm ....

3 Use the function machines to change

> 1 metre (m) = 100 centimetres (cm)

a metres into centimetres

b centimetres into metres.

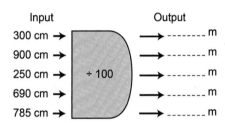

Input		Output
4 m →		→ .... cm
7 m →		→ .... cm
3.5 m →	× 100	→ .... cm
7.8 m →		→ .... cm
2.35 m →		→ .... cm

Input		Output
300 cm →		→ .... m
900 cm →		→ .... m
250 cm →	÷ 100	→ .... m
690 cm →		→ .... m
785 cm →		→ .... m

4 Real / Problem-solving   A parking space is 2200 mm wide.
Will a van of width 1.74 m fit in it, leaving room of 50 cm to open the door?

5 Write the missing number. Choose from 10, 100 or 1000.

> 1 kilometre (km) = 1000 metres (m)
> 1 kilogram (kg) = 1000 grams (g)
> 1 litre (*l*) = 1000 millilitres (m*l*)

a 1 litre = ... millilitres.

b There are .... millimetres in a centimetre.

c 1 kilogram = ... grams.

d There are .... metres in a kilometre.

e 1 metre = ... centimetres.

> **Worked example**
> [QR code]

6 Use the function machines to convert these units.

a

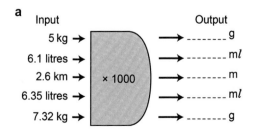

Input		Output
5 kg →		→ .... g
6.1 litres →		→ .... m*l*
2.6 km →	× 1000	→ .... m
6.35 litres →		→ .... m*l*
7.32 kg →		→ .... g

b

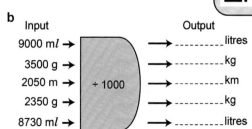

Input		Output
9000 m*l* →		→ .... litres
3500 g →		→ .... kg
2050 m →	÷ 1000	→ .... km
2350 g →		→ .... kg
8730 m*l* →		→ .... litres

CHECK   Tick each box as your **confidence** in this topic improves.

Need extra help? Go to page 65 and tick the boxes next to Q14–18. Then have a go at them once you've finished 6.1–6.7.

6.4 Adding and subtracting decimals

1 Write the next three terms in these decimal number sequences.

   a 0.3, 0.7, 1.1, ..., ..., ...

   b 3.5, 3.7, 3.9, ..., ..., ...

> What is being added on each time?
> Each sequence follows a rule.

2 Work out

   a 3.8 + 2.5   **b** 4.3 + 2.9   **c** 6.4 + 5.8

   ....

   d 6.8 − 3.5   **e** 7.2 − 4.8   **f** 9.5 − 2.7

   ....

> **Strategy hint**
> First add or subtract the whole
> number, and then the tenths.

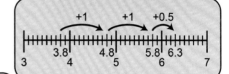

3 Work out

   a 23.4 + 18.9

```
  2 3 . 4
+ 1 8 . 9
─────────
      . 3
    1
```

> Set out the numbers so that they are in columns.
> Make sure the columns are lined up, tens with
> tens, units with units, tenths with tenths.
> Line up the decimal points.

> Start in the tenths column. Add the numbers together.
> 4 + 9 = 13. Put the 3 below the tenths and carry the 1.
> Write the 1 underneath the units column.

> Repeat for each column.
> Put the decimal point in the answer.

   b 21.8 + 35.6   **c** 15.8 + 42.5   **d** 38.4 + 25.6   **e** 183.6 kg + 42.7 kg

4 Work out

   a 75.8 − 43.6   **b** 54.1 − 25.6   **c** 243.6 − 56.7

> Line up the tens, units, tenths
> and the decimal points.
> ```
>   75.8
> − 43.6
> ──────
> ```

5 **Problem-solving** What is the total width of two parking spaces measuring 1.9 m each?

6 **Problem-solving** Brad weighs 31.2 kg and Tom weighs 29.7 kg.
How much heavier is Brad than Tom?

7 **Problem-solving** Alan buys a water butt for his garden. It has a capacity of 110 litres.
After a week of the rain, the water butt has collected 42.7 litres of water.
How much more water can the water butt hold?

CHECK Tick each box as your **confidence** in this topic improves.

Need extra help? Go to page 64 and tick the boxes next to Q8 and 9. Then have a go at them once you've finished 6.1–6.7.

1 Round these measurements to the nearest whole centimetre.
Use the ruler to help you.

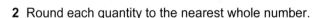

> For rounding to the nearest whole number, look at the tenths.
> • 0.5 and above round up.
> • 0.4 and below round down.
>
> rounds down   rounds up
>
> 7   7.5   8

a 5.3 cm .... **b** 7.7 cm .... **c** 2.6 cm .... **d** 11.5 cm ....

2 Round each quantity to the nearest whole number.

a 13.4 m .... **b** 4.8 kg .... **c** 52.71 km .... **d** £7.36 ....

> For rounding to 1 decimal place, look at the hundredths.
> • 0.05 and above round up.
> • 0.04 and below round down.
>
> rounds down   rounds up
>
> 3.1   3.15   3.2

3 For each measurement
  i write the measurement in metres   **ii** round to 1 decimal place.

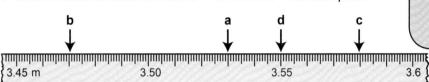

a i .... **b i** .... **c i** .... **d i** ....
  ii .... **ii** .... **ii** .... **ii** ....

4 Reasoning Circle the numbers that are written to 1 d.p.

5.24   6.2   42.7   9   3.0   35.79   6.2

> **Literacy hint**
> d.p. stands for 'decimal place'.

5 Round these decimals to the nearest tenth (1 decimal place).

a 7.96

> 7.96 rounds up to 8.
> Write 8.0 so there is 1 d.p.

  8.0

> Write the first decimal place, even if it is 0, to show you have rounded to 1 decimal place and not to the nearest whole number.

b 6.45   **c** 3.87   **d** 9.82   **e** 5.64

....

f 7.06   **g** 8.23   **h** 4.56   **i** 1.68

....

6 Work out each calculation. Write the answer on the calculator display.
Then round to 1 decimal place.

a 84 ÷ 25 .... **b** 325 ÷ 4 .... **c** 542 ÷ 8 ....

7 Problem-solving / Reasoning Mark rounds to the nearest whole number and gets 7.
Write three decimals that round to 7.

8 Finance Here is part of Freddie's receipt. Round each price to the nearest £.
Use your answers to work out an estimate for the total cost.

> RECEIPT
>
> £ 3.89
> £ 5.40
> £ 2.67
> £ 7.58
> £12.45
> =======

CHECK Tick each box as your **confidence** in this topic improves.

Need extra help? Go to page 64 and tick the boxes next to Q5 and 6. Then have a go at them once you've finished 6.1–6.7.

6.6 Multiplying and dividing decimals

1 Work out

a 0.4 × 2 .... **b** 0.6 × 3 .... **c** 7 × 0.2 .... **d** 8 × 0.3 ....

2 Work out

a 6.3 × 4

```
    6 3
  ×   4
  2 5 2
      1
```

63 × 4 = 252

6.3 × 4 = ...

> Ignore the decimal point and work out 63 × 4.
> 63 ÷ 10 = 6.3, so work out 252 ÷ 10 to get the answer.

b 4.3 × 9   **c** 7.6 × 8   **d** 6 × 5.2   **e** 4 × 8.5

> 6 × 5.2 is the same as 5.2 × 6

3 **Problem-solving** A recipe for a chocolate fudge cake needs 0.2 kg of plain chocolate.
How much chocolate is needed for 7 cakes?

> ☐ × 2 = 3.6

4 Work out

a 3.6 ÷ 2 .... **b** 2.8 ÷ 4 .... **c** 4.2 ÷ 7 .... **d** 5.4 ÷ 6 ....

5 Work out

a 53.1 ÷ 3

```
  1 ... . ...
3 ⟌ 5 ²3 . 1
```

> Look at the digits in 53.1, starting on the left.
> 3 goes into 5 once so write a 1 in the tens column above.
> The difference between 5 and 3 is 2, so write these 2 tens in the units column. to make 23.

```
  1 7 . ...
3 ⟌ 5 ²3 .²1
```

> 3 goes into 23 7 times with remainder 2 so write a 7 in the units column above. Write 2 units in the tenths column, to make 21 tenths.
> Write a decimal point in the answer.
> 3 goes into 21 7 times so write a 7 in the tenths column.

b 64.5 ÷ 5   **c** 71.4 ÷ 6   **d** 56.4 ÷ 4   **e** 76.2 ÷ 3

6 **Problem-solving** Olivia is working on an art project.
She makes 8 equal pieces of pipe cleaner from one of length 27.2 cm. How long is each piece?

7 **STEM** In a maths lesson, George is trying to work out the average weight of his 3 friends.
The total weight for the 3 friends is 97.8 kg. What is the average weight?

CHECK Tick each box as your **confidence** in this topic improves.

Need extra help? Go to pages 64–65 and tick the boxes next to Q10–11. Then have a go at them once you've finished 6.1 –6.7.

62

1 Real Work out the change from £10 for each amount.

a £8.65 .... b £3.50 .... c £1.99 .... d £4.25 ....

Count up to the next pound. Then count up to £10.

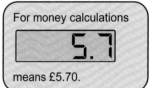

2 Problem-solving Amelia has been making bracelets and selling them. She sells bracelets for £1.50 each. Altogether she has taken £48. How many bracelets has she sold?

3 Reasoning Emily has 75 20p coins. She works out 75 × 20 = 1500. Ethan works out 75 × 0.20 = 15. Circle the answer which is in pounds.

4 Work out these amounts on a calculator.

a 6 × £1.25 .... b £10 − £4.60 ....

c £3.64 × 5 .... d £2.56 + £3.24 ....

e £10.40 ÷ 8 .... f £2.35 + £1.49 + £5.56 ....

For money calculations

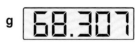

means £5.70.

5 Work out these on a calculator.
Write all the numbers on the display, then round to the nearest whole number.

a 542 ÷ 8 .... b 432 ÷ 5 .... c 531 ÷ 6 ....

6 Round the amounts of money on the calculator displays to the nearest penny (2 decimal places).

a **5.327**

5.327 £5.33

Look at the third decimal place (thousandths). It is a 7, so round up.

b **8.27495**

8.27495 £8.2....

The third decimal place is a 4, so round down.

c **26.99611**

26.99611 £27.00

The third decimal place is a 6, so round up.

d **40.555** e **12.999** f **31.651** g **68.307**

....

7 Work out the answer then round to the nearest penny.

a £257 ÷ 8 .... b £6.52 ÷ 5 ....

c £16 ÷ 3 .... d £265 ÷ 16 ....

8 Problem-solving A hospital needs to raise £7850 in one year for a new piece of equipment. How much will they need to raise each month? Give your answer to the nearest penny.

CHECK Tick each box as your **confidence** in this topic improves.

Need extra help? Go to page 64 and tick the box next to Q7. Then have a go at it once you've finished 6.1–6.7.

6 Strengthen

Decimal numbers

1 Write each number into the place-value table.
What is the value of the 3 in each number?

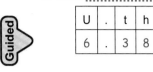

a 6.38 ....

U	.	t	h
6	.	3	8

b 3.09 ....

U	.	t	h
	.		

c 5.73 ....

U	.	t	h
	.		

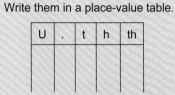

Is the 3 in the units (U), tenths (t) or hundredths (h) column?

2 Circle the numbers which have the same value.

4.01   4.1   4.10   44.10   4.100

Write them in a place-value table.

U	.	t	h	th
	.			

3 Compare these pairs of numbers. Write < or > between each pair.

a 7.46 .... 7.64

U	.	t	h
7	.	4	6
7	.	6	4

They both have 7 units, but 7.64 has more tenths.

b 3.41 .... 3.08

U	.	t	h
	.		
	.		

c 2.4 .... 2.05

U	.	t	h
	.		
	.		

Write both numbers in the place-value tables. Work from left to right.

Compare the digits, starting with the units.

4 Write these decimals in order, smallest first.

6.23   6.33   6.32   6.22 ....

5 Round these numbers to the nearest whole number.

a 4.8 ....   **b** 7.3 ....   **c** 6.5 ....

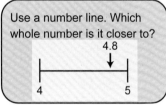

Use a number line. Which whole number is it closer to?

6 Round these numbers to 1 decimal place.

a 1.36 ....   **b** 6.54 ....   **c** 8.25 ....

7 **Real / Finance**   Rayan earns £12.50 an hour.
How much does he earn for a 6-hour shift?

8 Work out

a 1.3 + 2.5 ....

b 4.6 + 3.8 ....

c 2.7 + 6.9 ....

Split one of the units in 5.2 into 10 tenths

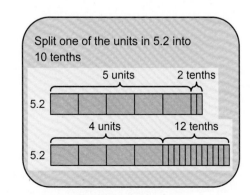

9 Work out

a 7.6 – 4.3 ....

b 5.2 – 1.8 ....

c 7.4 – 2.5 ....

10 a Work out   **i** 6 × 9 _____   **ii** 6 × 0.9 _____

  b What do you notice? _____

  c 8 × 6 = 48. What is 8 × 0.6? _____

  d 7 × 12 = 84. What is 0.7 × 12? _____

11 a Work out   **i** 63 ÷ 9 _____   **ii** 6.3 ÷ 9 _____

  b What do you notice? _____

  c 32 ÷ 4 = 8. What is 3.2 ÷ 4? _____

  d 42 ÷ 6 = 7. What is 4.2 ÷ 7? _____

Measurements and scales

What measurement do the small marks represent?

12 Write these measurements. Write the number and the units.

  a

  cm 80 85

  b **c**

  0 cm 1 2 3 4

  a _____
  b _____
  c _____

13 Write these measurements to 2 decimal places.

  a **b**

  m 3.5 3.6 3.7 3.8 3.9 4

  a _____
  b _____

14 Use a double number line to convert between centimetres and millimetres.

Guided

  a 3 cm = _____ × 10 = _____ mm   **b** 7.5 cm = _____ mm

  c 60 mm = _____ ÷ 10 = _____ cm   **d** 23 mm = _____ cm

  cm 1 2 3
  ×10 (|——|——|——|) ÷10
  mm 10 20 □

15 Use a double number line to convert between centimetres and metres.

Guided

  a 5 m = _____ × 100 = _____ cm   **b** 4.28 m = _____ cm

  c 700 cm = _____ ÷ 100 = _____ m   **d** 430 cm = _____ m

  m 1 2 3
  ×100 (|——|——|——|) ÷100
  cm 100 200 □

16 Use the double number lines to work out these conversions.

  kg 1 2   litres 1 2   metres 1 2
  |——|——| |——|——| |——|——|
  g 1000 2000   ml 1000 2000   mm 1000 2000

  a 4 m = _____ mm   **b** 6 kg = _____ g   **c** 5.6 litres = _____ ml

  d 8000 ml = _____ litres   **e** 2500 g = _____ kg   **f** 9800 mm = _____ m

17 Compare these measurements. Write < or > between each pair.

Guided

  a 250 cm _____ 3 m

  3 m = 3 × 100 = 300 cm

  Convert to the same units.
  Now compare 250 cm and 300 cm. 250 < 300

  Convert the measurements to the same units.

  b 7.2 litres _____ 7100 ml   **c** 8 cm _____ 77 mm   **d** 8300 g _____ 8.5 kg

18 Write these measurements in order, smallest first.

  66 cm   6 m   6 cm   6.6 m _____

1 Reasoning   Work out the missing numbers in these sequences.

   a   3.5, 5.0, ..., ..., 9.5

   b   9.6, 9.0, ..., ..., 7.2

> The same amount is added or subtracted each time.

2 Reasoning   Work out the missing numbers in these sequences.

   a   2.4, ..., ..., ..., 4.0

   b   8.3, ..., ..., ..., 5.5

3   Round these prices to the nearest 10p.

   a   £5.32 ....   **b**   £8.75 ....   **c**   £1.99 ....

4   Round these lengths to the nearest mm.

   a   4.26 cm ....   **b**   36.529 cm ....

   c   0.57 cm ....   **d**   14.0429 cm ....

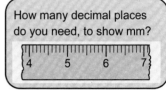

> How many decimal places do you need, to show mm?

5 Reasoning   Here are two calculations that Nadia did for homework.
Explain the mistake she has made in each calculation.
Do each calculation correctly.

   a
```
  5 3 . 2
+    4 . 1
─────────
  9 4 . 2
```
   b
```
  8 2 . 3
-  2 6 . 8
─────────
  6 4 . 5
```

6   Convert between these measures.

   a   5.2 litres = ... m*l*   **b**   0.54 kg = ... g

   c   740 m = ... km   **d**   38 mm = ... cm

> Do you need to multiply or divide?

7 Problem-solving   The Riley family's suitcases are being weighed at the airport.
The scales show the mass of each suitcase.
How much do their suitcases weigh altogether? ....

8   Work out

   a   5.72 + 6.79 ....   **b**   6.41 − 3.45 ....   **c**   24.7 − 8.53 ....

```
  5.72
+ 6.79
──────
```

9 Work out

   a 37.2 × 8 ....   **b** 7 × 246.3 ....   **c** 574.2 ÷ 9 ....

10 Real   Isaac is touring Australia with his family.
They travel from Perth to Alice Springs, and then to Sydney.

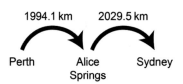

1994.1 km   2029.5 km

Perth   Alice   Sydney
Springs

   a What is the total distance they will travel from Perth to Sydney?

   b Round the two distances to the nearest km and add them.

   c What is the difference between the rounded distance and the actual distance?

   d The shortest distance between Perth and Sydney is 3294.1 km.
How many more kilometres is the journey going via Alice Springs?

11 Real / Problem-solving   A professional runner took 9.63 seconds to complete a 100 m race and
19.32 seconds to complete a 200 m race.
Did it take him twice as long to run twice the distance?

> **Literacy hint**
> Decimals where the
> digits repeat are called
> recurring decimals.

 12 Use a calculator. Write down all the numbers on the display, then round
to the nearest pound.

   a £5497 ÷ 5 ....   **b** £6491 ÷ 3 ....   **c** £2572 ÷ 12 ....

13 Round each calculator display to give an answer in pounds and pence.

   a 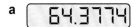 64.3774   **b** 31.12935   **c** 3.33333

....

   d  8.66666   **e** 45.55555   **f** 18.9999

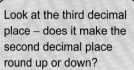

> Look at the third decimal
> place – does it make the
> second decimal place
> round up or down?

....

 14 15 m of ribbon costs £22. How much is that per metre, to the nearest penny?

15 Reasoning   Esme and five friends celebrate her birthday by going out for a meal.
The total restaurant bill is £77.65.
Esme says that they need to pay £13 each.
Molly says it should be £12.94.
Rose says that they need to pay £12.95.
Who is right? Explain your answer.

> **PROGRESS BAR** Colour in the progress bar as you get questions correct.
> Then fill in the progression chart on pages 111–113.

1 Write down these measurements.

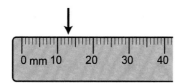

a ....

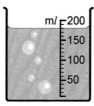

b ....

2 Estimate the mass shown on this scale. ....

3 Measure this line. ───────────

4 What is the value of the 2 in each of these numbers?

a 46.27 ....   b 29.01 ....

c 90.12 ....   d 62.53 ....

5 What is the change from £10 for each amount?

a £6.25 ....   b £1.95 ....   c £8.65 ....

6 Write these in order, smallest first.   3.5   5.3   3.15   3.41   3.1

7 Work out

a 3.4 + 7.8   b 7.3 − 2.8   c 35.6 + 84.9   d 145.2 − 68.7

8 How much shorter is 34.7 m than 82.5 m?

9 Convert these units.

a 4.7 kg = ... g   b 5870 m = ... km   c 45 mm = ... cm

10 Write these measures in order, smallest first.   5.68 litres   5500 m*l*   5.55 litres

11 Round each number to the nearest whole number.

a 6.3 ....   b 4.65 ....   c 7.5 ....

12 Round each number to the nearest 1 decimal place.

a 5.34..............   b 3.67 ....   c 7.85 ....

13 A pack of 24 felt-tip pens costs £4.99.
How much does one felt-tip pen cost, to the nearest penny?

1 Circle the right angles.

a 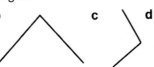 **b** **c** **d**

> Angle measures a turn. Angles are measured in degrees (°).
> A whole turn is 360°. A half turn is 180°.
>
>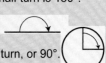
>
> A right angle is a quarter turn, or 90°.

2 Mark any right angles on these shapes, using the right angle symbol.

a  **b** **c**

> A corner of a piece of paper is a right angle. To check an angle, see if the corner fits exactly.

> This symbol means an angle is a right angle.

3 Write if these turns are clockwise or anticlockwise.

a **b** **c** **d**

....

> The direction of a turn is either clockwise or anticlockwise.
>
> clockwise   anticlockwise

4 Look at each turn. Write if it is clockwise or anticlockwise and if it is a $\frac{1}{4}$, $\frac{1}{2}$ or $\frac{3}{4}$ turn.

a **b** **c** **d**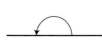

....

5 a Complete this compass.

b What direction would you be facing after following each of these instructions?

W = ...°

E = ...°

S = ...°

N = 0°

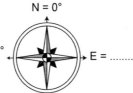

i Start facing N and turn clockwise through 180°. ....

ii Start facing S and turn clockwise through 90°. ....

iii Start facing W and turn anticlockwise through 270°. ....

> You can use a compass to give directions.
> Angles on a compass are measured clockwise from north.
>
> north
> north-west   north-east
> west   east
> south-west   south-east
> south

6 Look at these pairs of lines. Write if they are perpendicular, parallel or neither.

a **b** **c** **d**

....

> Perpendicular lines meet at right angles (90°). Parallel lines are always the same distance apart and never meet.

7 Look at these shapes.

a Show any parallel lines using arrows.

b Show any right angles using the right angle symbol.

> Use > to show one set of parallel lines.
> Use ≫ to show a different set of parallel lines.

 Guided

i 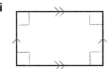 **ii** **iii** **iv**  **v**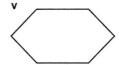

CHECK Tick each box as your **confidence** in this topic improves. ☹ 😐 🙂

Need extra help? Go to page 74 and tick the boxes next to Q1, 4 and 5. Then have a go at them once you've finished 7.1–7.5.

69

1 Measure and label these angles.

a

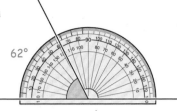

62°

b

c

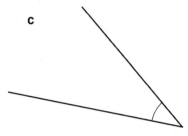

> Place the protractor on the point of the angle.
> Line up the zero line with one line of the angle.
> Read up from 0.

> Decide which scale to use by
> reading up from 0 each time.

2 For each angle write if it is acute or obtuse.

a

b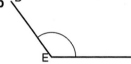

c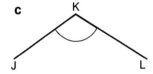

d

....

3 The shape ABCD is a parallelogram. Write down the names for

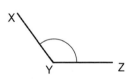

> An acute angle is
> smaller than 90°.
> An obtuse angle is
> between 90° and 180°.

a the line parallel to AB ....

b the diagonal of the parallelogram ....

c the two shorter sides of the parallelogram. .... and ....

> Line AB joins A and B.

4 Write down the name of each of these angles.

a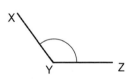

b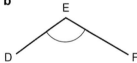

c

....

> The diagram shows
> ∠XYZ.
> The angle is always
> at the middle letter.
> It can also be written
> as XŶZ.
>
>

5 Look at the parallelogram in Q3. Write down the name of the angle where

a line AB meets BD ....

b line BC meets CD ....

c line AD meets BD. ....

6 **Problem-solving** The diagram shows an isosceles triangle.

a Measure ∠BAC. ....

b How big do you think AĈB is? ....

Measure to check your answer.

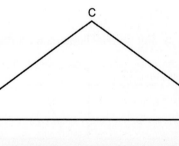

CHECK   Tick each box as your **confidence** in this topic improves.

Need extra help? Go to pages 74–75 and tick the boxes next to Q2, 3, 9 and 10. Then have a go at them once you've finished 7.1–7.5.

1 For each angle write if it is acute, obtuse or reflex.

a

b

c

....

> The angle on a straight line is 180°. An angle larger than 180° is a reflex angle. A reflex angle is more than 180°, but less than 360°.
>
> ↘ 180°

2 Measure and label these angles.

Guided

a 135°

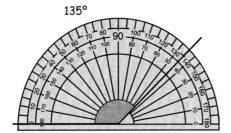

> Place the protractor on the point of the angle. Line up the zero line with one line of the angle. Read up from 0.

Worked example

b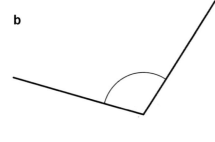

c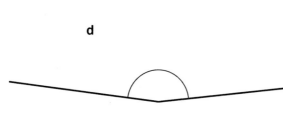

d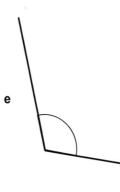

e

3 Problem-solving The diagram shows a regular pentagon.

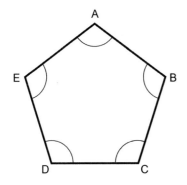

> Make sure you use the correct scale. Check your answer is reasonable. An obtuse angle is between 90° and 180°.

a Measure ∠ABC. ....

b How big do you think CD̂E is? ....

Measure to check your answer.

CHECK Tick each box as your **confidence** in this topic improves.

Need extra help? Go to pages 74–75 and tick the boxes next to Q6 and 9. Then have a go at them once you've finished 7.1–7.5.

1   **i** Estimate the size of each angle.   **ii** Check your answers by measuring.

a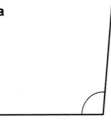

b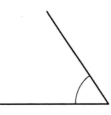

c

i ....

ii ....

i ....

ii ....

i ....

ii ....

Worked example

2   Use a ruler and protractor to draw these angles accurately.

a
3 cm
80°
5 cm

b
3 cm
25°   4.5 cm

c
5.5 cm
33°
6.5 cm

Use a ruler to draw a 5 cm line.

Place the protractor on the 5 cm line with the cross exactly on one end. Start at 0 and read up to 80°. Mark this point with a pencil.

Use a ruler to draw a 3 cm line from the point of the angle towards the mark. Label the angle and lines with the correct measurements.

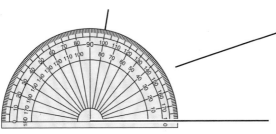

CHECK   Tick each box as your **confidence** in this topic improves.

Need extra help? Go to pages 74–75 and tick the boxes next to Q7, 8 and 11. Then have a go at them once you've finished 7.1–7.5.

1 Work out the size of the unknown angles.

a

$m = 180° - 130°$

= ....

b

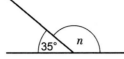

$n =$ ....

= ....

c

....

> The angles on a straight line add up to 180°.
>
>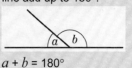
>
> $a + b = 180°$

d

....

e

....

f

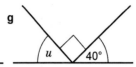

....

g

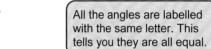

....

2 Problem-solving / Reasoning Work out the size of angle x.

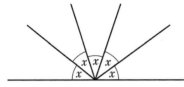

$x =$ ....

> All the angles are labelled with the same letter. This tells you they are all equal.

3 Problem-solving / Reasoning

a Work out the size of angle x.

b Work out the size of angle y.

c Work out the sum of angles round a point.

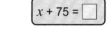

$x + 75 = \square$

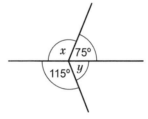

4 Work out the size of the unknown angles.

a

....

b

....

c

....

> The angles round a point add up to 360°.
>
>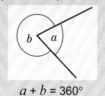
>
> $a + b = 360°$

5 Work out the size of ∠ABC in each of these diagrams.

a

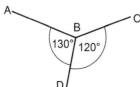

b

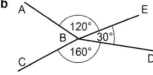

a ....

b ....

CHECK   Tick each box as your **confidence** in this topic improves.

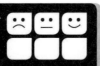

Need extra help? Go to page 75 and tick the boxes next to Q12 and 13. Then have a go at them once you've finished 7.1–7.5.

73

7 Strengthen

Types of angles and lines

1 The angle in **a** is a right angle. Circle the angle in **b** to **e** that is *not* a right angle.

  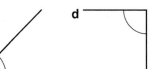

a   b   c   d   e

> You make a right angle when you sit upright.

2 Circle the acute angles.

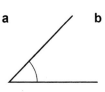 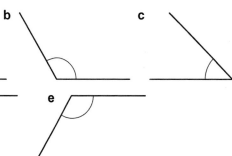

a   b   c

d   e

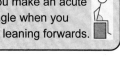

> You make an acute angle when you sit leaning forwards.

3 Which of the angles in Q2 are obtuse? ....

> You make an obtuse angle when you sit leaning backwards.

4 Circle the pairs of parallel lines.

a   b   c   d

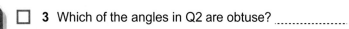
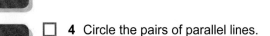

> Imagine making the lines longer. Parallel lines will never cross.

5 Circle the pairs of perpendicular lines.

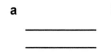

a   b   c   d

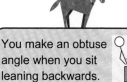

> Perpendicular lines make a right angle. You can remember this using PERPENDICU⌐AR

 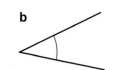

6 Circle the reflex angle.

a   b   c   d

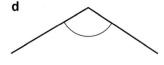

   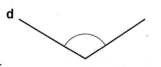

Estimating, measuring and drawing angles

7 Jordan measures an angle. He says, 'This angle measures 145°'.
Clare says, 'It can't be. It is smaller than a right angle.'
Explain what Jordan has done wrong.

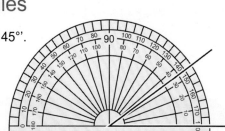

8 Circle the correct measurement for each of these angles.

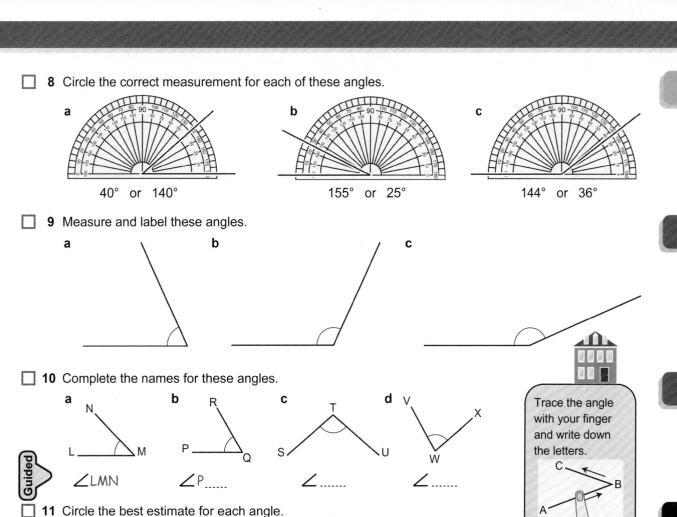

a   40° or 140°

b   155° or 25°

c   144° or 36°

9 Measure and label these angles.

a

b

c

10 Complete the names for these angles.

Trace the angle with your finger and write down the letters.

a 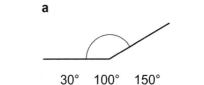 ∠LMN

b 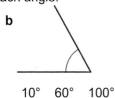 ∠P......

c 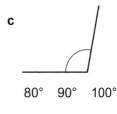 ∠ ....

d 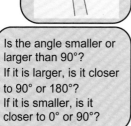 ∠ ....

11 Circle the best estimate for each angle.

a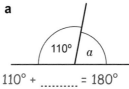

30° 100° 150°

b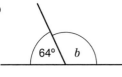

10° 60° 100°

c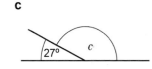

80° 90° 100°

Is the angle smaller or larger than 90°?
If it is larger, is it closer to 90° or 180°?
If it is smaller, is it closer to 0° or 90°?

Calculating angles

12 Work out the size of the unknown angles. Explain your reason.

a
110° a

110° + ... = 180°

a = ...

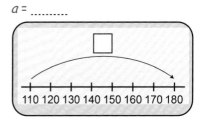

110 120 130 140 150 160 170 180

b
64° b

c
27° c

13 Work out the size of the unknown angles. Explain your reason.

a
x
285°

285° + ... = 360°

x = ...

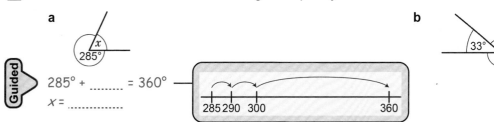

285 290 300   360

b
33°
y

75

1 Look at the compass.
Write the angle between

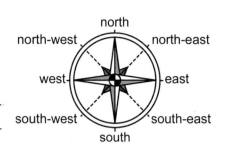

north

a east and west ....

b north and east ....

c south-east and south-west ....

d north-east and south-west. ....

Worked example

2 Real   An aircraft is heading north.
It travels for 150 miles and then turns through 225° clockwise to continue the journey.
Which direction is the aircraft now travelling in?

3 For each shape, write down the number of

i right angles   **ii** pairs of parallel lines   **iii** pairs of perpendicular sides.

a

b

c

a i ....
ii ....
iii ....

b i ....
ii ....
iii ....

c i ....
ii ....
iii ....

4 a Measure

i line AB ....

ii angle BCD ....

iii line EF ....

iv AĜF ....

b Write down the number of each type of angle in the shape.

i acute angles ....

ii obtuse angles ....

iii reflex angles ....

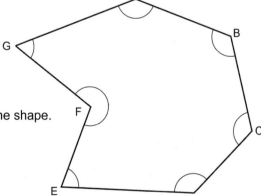

5 Reasoning   Work out the size of these angles.

a angle q is twice the size of angle p

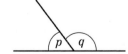

b angle t is four times the size of angle s

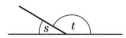

6 Real / Reasoning

a What angle does the minute hand of a clock turn through in

i 30 minutes .... ii $\frac{1}{4}$ hour .... iii 10 minutes? ....

b What angle does the second hand of a clock turn through in

i 2 minutes .... ii 15 seconds .... iii 45 seconds? ....

c What angle does the hour hand of a clock turn through in

i 9 hours .... ii 10 hours .... iii 4 hours? ....

7 Reasoning Work out the size of these angles.

a angle x is three times the size of angle w

b angle z is five times the size of angle y

8 a Draw the triangle accurately using a ruler and protractor.

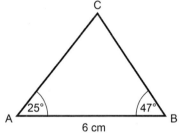

Draw the line AB first. Next measure and draw the angles.

Worked example

b Measure

i AC .... ii BC .... iii ∠ACB ....

9 Problem-solving / Reasoning The diagram shows two of the corners of a rectangle.
List as many different coordinates for the third and fourth corners of the rectangle as possible.

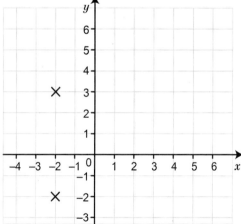

10 Draw ∠ABC = 64°.

PROGRESS BAR Colour in the progress bar as you get questions correct. Then fill in the progression chart on pages 111–113.

1 Circle the right angles.

a   b   c   d

2 a How many acute angles are in triangle ABC? ....

b Measure the length of the line AB. ....

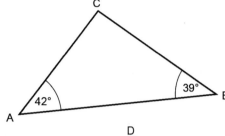

3 The diagram shows a quadrilateral.

a What is the size of angle DAB? ....

b Is ∠ABC acute or obtuse? ....

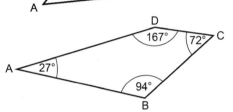

4 Write below each pair of lines whether they are parallel, perpendicular or neither.

a    b   c   d

....

5 Look at the diagram.

a Label each angle as acute (A), obtuse (O) or reflex (R).

b Measure

   i ∠PQR ....

   ii angle QRS ....

   iii PT̂S ....

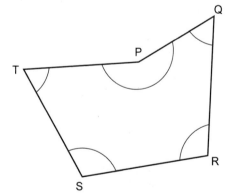

6 Draw this angle accurately.

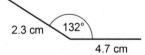

7 Work out the size of the unknown angles.

a   b

a ....

b ....

8.1 Shapes

1 Measure the sides and angles of each triangle.
Write down if it is scalene, isosceles or equilateral.

a

b

c

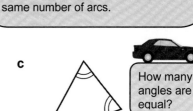

scalene   isosceles   equilateral

all angles and sides different   two equal angles and sides   all angles and sides equal

- The number of equal sides and angles can help you identify a triangle.
- Equal sides are marked using a dash.
- Equal angles are shown using the same number of arcs.

....

2 For each triangle write down if it is scalene, isosceles or equilateral.

a

'Same arcs' means 'same angles'.

b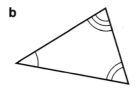

c

How many angles are equal?

Equilateral ....

3 Circle the quadrilaterals.

A   B   C   D

  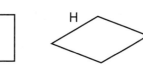

E   F   G   H

- A quadrilateral is a flat shape with four straight sides.
- Squares and rectangles are special quadrilaterals. All their corners are right angles.

square   rectangle

all sides equal   opposite sides equal

4 a On the square grid, draw a square with 3 cm sides.
Mark the equal sides using dashes. Mark the four right angles.

b Join two opposite corners to make a diagonal.

c Measure the diagonal to the nearest millimetre. ....

d Draw and measure the other diagonal.

What do you notice? ....

e Complete the sentence:

The diagonals of a square are ....

5 a Draw a rectangle with sides 7 cm and 4 cm.

b Draw its diagonals and measure them.

....

c Complete the sentence:

The diagonals of a rectangle are ....

d Measure the angles between the diagonals.
Use arcs to mark any that are equal.

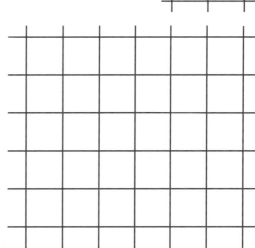

Need extra help? Go to page 85 and tick the box next to Q2. Then have a go at it once you've finished 8.1–8.6.

8.2 Symmetry in shapes

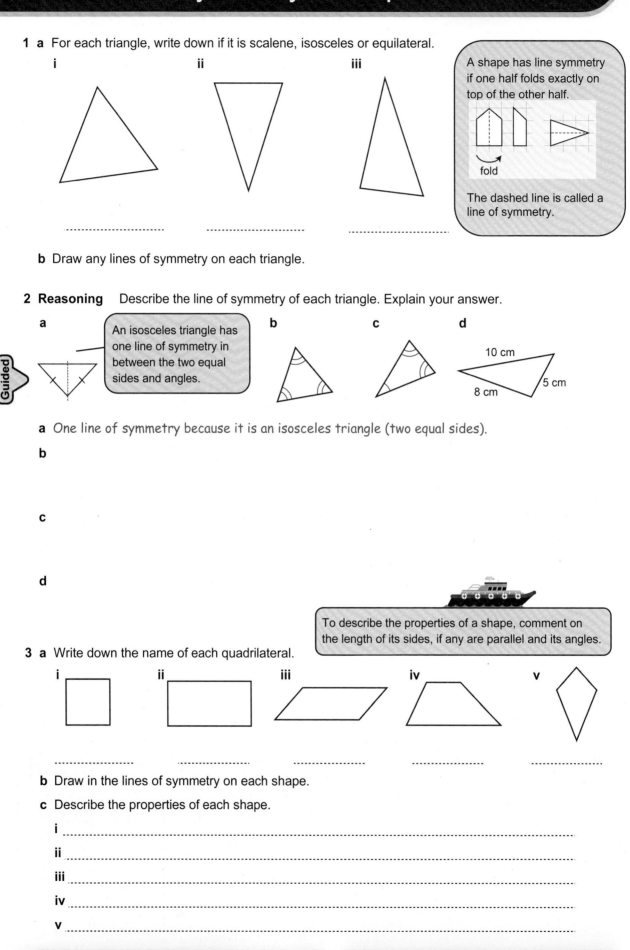

1 a For each triangle, write down if it is scalene, isosceles or equilateral.

i

ii

iii

> A shape has line symmetry if one half folds exactly on top of the other half.
>
> fold
>
> The dashed line is called a line of symmetry.

....

b Draw any lines of symmetry on each triangle.

2 Reasoning   Describe the line of symmetry of each triangle. Explain your answer.

Guided

a

> An isosceles triangle has one line of symmetry in between the two equal sides and angles.

b   **c**   **d**

10 cm

5 cm

8 cm

a One line of symmetry because it is an isosceles triangle (two equal sides).

b

c

d

> To describe the properties of a shape, comment on the length of its sides, if any are parallel and its angles.

3 a Write down the name of each quadrilateral.

i   ii   iii   iv   v

....

b Draw in the lines of symmetry on each shape.

c Describe the properties of each shape.

i ....

ii ....

iii ....

iv ....

v ....

CHECK   Tick each box as your **confidence** in this topic improves.   ☹ 😐 🙂

Need extra help? Go to page 85 and tick the box next to Q3. Then have a go at it once you've finished 8.1–8.6.

1 a Find the missing lengths and angles in these triangles.

i

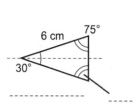

6 cm 75°
30°

ii

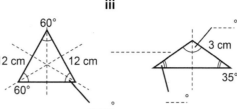

60°
12 cm 12 cm
60°

iii

3 cm
35°

The dashed lines are lines of symmetry.
One half fits exactly on top of the other half.

b Name each triangle. Give a reason for your answer.

i Isosceles

Reason: Two sides are equal and two angles are equal.

ii ....

Reason: ....

iii ....

Reason: ....

2 Find the order of rotational symmetry for each shape.

A   **B**   **C**   **D**

....

A shape has rotational symmetry if it looks the same more than once in a full turn.

The shape looks the same in three positions, so it has rotational symmetry of order 3.

3 For each shape work out

i the order of rotational symmetry

ii the number of lines of symmetry.

Trace the shape and turn it through a full turn. How many times does the shape look the same as you turn? Only count the starting position once.

A   **B**   **C**

i ....   **i** ....   **i** ....

ii ....   **ii** ....   **ii** ....

Worked example

D   **E**   **F**

i ....   **i** ....   **i** ....

ii ....   **ii** ....   **ii** ....

8.4 Regular polygons

1 Write down how many sides each polygon has.

a Octagon .... **b** Pentagon .... **c** Decagon ....

d Hexagon .... **e** Nonagon .... **f** Heptagon ....

> A polygon is a 2D shape with straight sides. A regular polygon has equal sides and equal angles.

2 a Write the name of each shape.

b Tick the regular polygons.

> Are all of the sides and angles equal?

i .... **ii** .... **iii** .... **iv** ....

v .... **vi** .... **vii** .... **viii** ....

3 a How many lines of symmetry does a regular pentagon have? ....

b What is the order of rotational symmetry of a regular pentagon? ....

Guided

a .... lines of symmetry

b rotational symmetry of order ....

> How many ways can you fold a pentagon in half?

> Rotate the pentagon a full turn. In how many positions does it look the same?

4 a Draw the lines of symmetry on this regular octagon.

b How many lines of symmetry does it have? ....

c What is the order of rotational symmetry of a regular octagon? ....

d Complete this table.

Regular polygon	pentagon	hexagon	heptagon	octagon	nonagon	decagon
Lines of symmetry						
Order of rotational symmetry						

5 Problem solving Sketch a polygon with

a 2 lines of symmetry and 8 sides

b 1 line of symmetry and 7 sides.

CHECK Tick each box as your **confidence** in this topic improves.

Need extra help? Go to page 85 and tick the boxes next to Q1 and 3. Then have a go at them once you've finished 8.1–8.6.

1 a Write the other side lengths on this square.

b Work out the perimeter.

7cm

> The perimeter is the total distance around the edge of a shape. Add the lengths of all the sides to work out the perimeter of a shape.

 2 A square lawn has a side of 5.6 m. Work out its perimeter.

> **Strategy hint**
> Sketch and label the square.

3 a Write the other side lengths on this rectangle.

b Work out the perimeter.

6 cm

2 cm

 4 Real A sheet of A4 paper measures 29.7 cm by 21 cm. Work out its perimeter.

> **Guided**

Perimeter = 29.7 + 29.7 + ... + ... = ... cm

> A4 paper is a rectangle. Opposite sides of a rectangle are equal.

5 a Label the other sides of this regular hexagon.

b Work out the perimeter.

3 cm

6 Real 'The Pentagon' in Washington DC, USA, is the world's largest office block. Each outside wall measures 280 metres in length.
Find the perimeter of the Pentagon.

> 'The Pentagon' is a regular pentagon.

7 These shapes have been made by joining rectangles together.

A

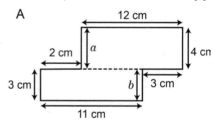

12 cm

2 cm a

3 cm b 3 cm   4 cm

11 cm

B

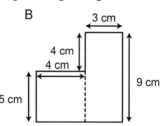

3 cm

4 cm
4 cm

5 cm

9 cm

C

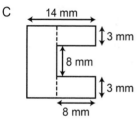

14 mm

3 mm

8 mm

3 mm

8 mm

a For shape A, write down the length of

i side a ....   **ii** side b. ....

b Work out the perimeter of shape A.

c Work out the perimeter of shape B.

d Work out the perimeter of shape C.

CHECK Tick each box as your **confidence** in this topic improves.

Need extra help? Go to pages 86–87 and tick the boxes next to Q5, 6, 10 and 11. Then have a go at them once you've finished 8.1–8.6.

1 Work out the area of each rectangle.

a area = length × width

= 12 cm × .... cm

= .... cm²

12 cm
9 cm

> Area is the space inside a shape.
> Area is measured using square units.
>
> 1 cm
> 1 cm
>
> One square centimetre = 1 cm².

b
9 cm
7 cm

c
3 cm
12 cm

....

> Area of a rectangle = length × width

2 Real A sheet of A4 paper measures 29.7 cm by 21 cm.
Find the area of a sheet of A4 paper.

> A square millimetre (mm²) is the area of a square of side 1 mm.
>
> □ This is the actual size (of 1 square millimetre)

3 a Write the square unit best used to describe the area of each of these objects: cm² or mm².

b Estimate the area of each object.

i

smartphone

Unit: ....

Estimate of area: ....

ii
K₅
SCRABBLE® letter

Unit: ....

Estimate of area: ....

iii
tablet

Unit: ....

Estimate of area: ....

4 Problem-solving A square has a side of 8 cm.
A rectangle has a width of 7 cm and a length of 9 cm.
Which shape has the greater area?

5 These shapes are made by joining two rectangles together.
Work out the area of each shape.

a
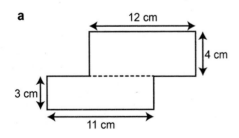
12 cm
4 cm
3 cm
11 cm

b
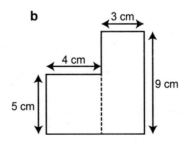
3 cm
4 cm
9 cm
5 cm

Worked example

> Work out the area of each rectangle. Add the answers together.

CHECK Tick each box as your **confidence** in this topic improves.

Need extra help? Go to pages 86–87 and tick the boxes next to Q7–11. Then have a go at them once you've finished 8.1–8.6.

Shapes

1 a Match each shape with its name.

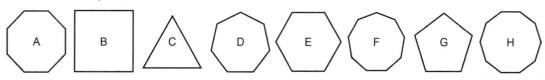

Triangle *C* Square .... Pentagon .... Hexagon .... | Count the sides. |

Heptagon .... Octagon .... Nonagon .... Decagon ....

b Which shape is a type of quadrilateral? ....

2 The diagram shows two equilateral triangles, two isosceles triangles and two scalene triangles.
Draw lines to join each triangle on the left with the same type of triangle on the right.

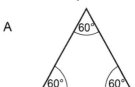

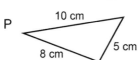

Look at the first four letters.
• equi – like 'equal' – all angles and sides equal.
• isos – two letters the same – two angles and sides the same.
• scal – all letters different – all angles and sides different.

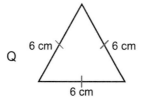

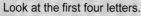

Which of A to C is the equilateral? Join it to the other equilateral triangle.

Symmetry

3 a Draw a line of symmetry on each shape. Check your line using a mirror.

Place a mirror upright along your mirror line. Do you see the original shape?

....

b Draw any other lines of symmetry for each shape.

c Write the number of lines of symmetry beneath each shape.

4 a Trace each shape, including the dot.

When rotating, count the number of times the traced shape fits the original. Only count the starting position once.

....

b Hold your pencil on the dot. Rotate the traced shape a full turn. How many times does it look the same? Write the order of rotational symmetry beneath each shape.

Perimeter and area

☐ **5** The rectangles below are drawn on centimetre squared paper.

   a Find the perimeter of each shape by counting the squares on all four sides.
Write your answer beneath each shape.

i   **ii**   **iii**

4 cm

....

   b Write the length of each side on the diagram. What do you notice about opposite sides?

   c Add the lengths together to find the perimeter of each shape. Is it the same as in part **a**?

☐ **6 a** Write the lengths of the other two sides on each rectangle below.

   b Work out the perimeter of each rectangle.

i 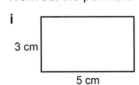   **ii** 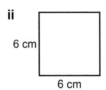   **iii**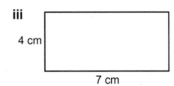

Perimeter = 5 + 3 + ... + ...

            = ... cm

> Add the measurements of
> all four sides together.

☐ **7** These shapes are drawn on centimetre squared paper.
Find the area of each shape by counting squares.

a   **b**   **c**

»»»»»

> Each square on
> centimetre squared
> paper has area 1 cm².

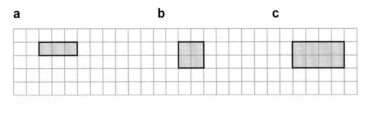

....

☐ **8** These rectangles are drawn on centimetre squared paper.
For each rectangle write down

   i how many squares are in each row

   ii how many rows there are

   iii how many squares altogether

   iv the area of the rectangle.

> 5 rows of 2 squares is
> 5 × 2 = 10

a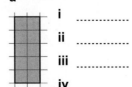

   i ....
   ii ....
   iii ....
   iv ....

b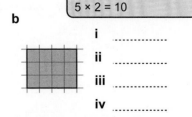

   i ....
   ii ....
   iii ....
   iv ....

9 Use the length and width to calculate the area of each rectangle.

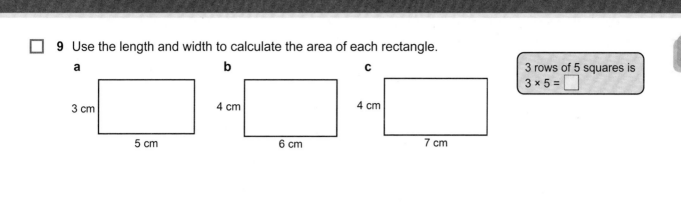

a

3 cm

5 cm

b

4 cm

6 cm

c

4 cm

7 cm

3 rows of 5 squares is
3 × 5 = ☐

10 These shapes are drawn on centimetre squared paper.
Each shape is made by joining two rectangles.

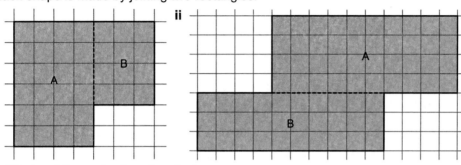

i

B

A

ii

A

B

a Work out the perimeter of each shape.

For perimeter, count the
squares around the outside.

b Find the total area of each shape.

Total area = area of rectangle A + area of rectangle B

11 Each shape is made by joining two rectangles.

a Work out the perimeter of each shape.

b Work out the total area of each shape.

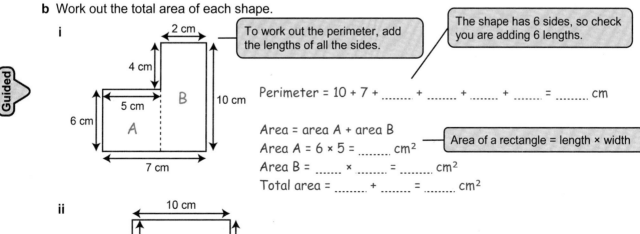

i

2 cm

4 cm

5 cm

B

A

6 cm

10 cm

7 cm

To work out the perimeter, add
the lengths of all the sides.

The shape has 6 sides, so check
you are adding 6 lengths.

Perimeter = 10 + 7 + ... + ... + ... + ... = ... cm

Area = area A + area B
Area A = 6 × 5 = ... cm²
Area B = ... × .... = ... cm²
Total area = ... + ... = ... cm²

Area of a rectangle = length × width

ii

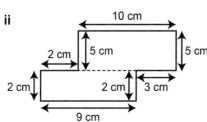

10 cm

2 cm

5 cm

5 cm

2 cm

2 cm

3 cm

9 cm

Guided

87

1 Problem-solving The diagram shows four regular polygons.

4 cm

3 cm

2 cm

The sum of the perimeters of the triangle and octagon is equal to the sum of the perimeters of the hexagon and square.
Work out the side length of the square.

2 A floor of a room has a width of 3.8 m and a perimeter of 16.2 m.
Work out the length of the floor.

Strategy hint
You may want to sketch a diagram to help you.

3 Problem-solving The diagram shows a rectangular picture frame.
The width of the picture frame is 50 cm.
The perimeter of the picture frame is 220 cm.
Work out the height of the picture frame.

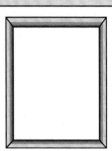

4 Problem-solving A square swimming pool has perimeter 33 m.
Work out the side length of the swimming pool.

5 a Name a quadrilateral that has rotational symmetry of order 4.

b Name two quadrilaterals that have rotational symmetry of order 2.

6 STEM These four shapes are capital letters from the Greek alphabet. Mathematicians often use the letters from the Greek alphabet.

i   ii   iii   iv

Phi   Sigma   Delta   Xi

Mathematicians often use the letters from the Greek alphabet.

a How many lines of symmetry does each shape have?

i ....   ii ....   iii ....   iv ....

b What is the order of rotational symmetry of each shape?

i ....   ii ....   iii ....   iv ....

7 This pattern is made using tiles of two regular polygons.

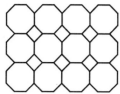

Complete this table for the two shapes.

Name of shape		
Number of lines of symmetry		
Order of rotational symmetry		

8 Finance This is the floor plan of a house.

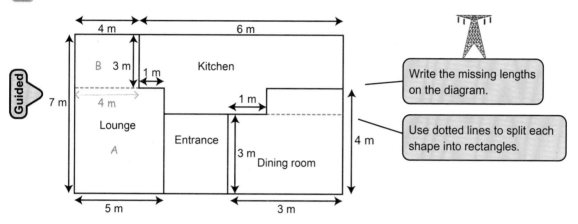

Write the missing lengths on the diagram.

Use dotted lines to split each shape into rectangles.

a Work out the floor area for each room in the house.

Lounge   Entrance

Area A = 5 × 4 = ... m²

Area B = 3 × 4 = ... m²

Lounge area = ... + ... = ... m²

Kitchen   Dining room

b The carpet for the lounge costs £16 per square metre.
Work out the total cost of the carpet for the lounge.

c The floor tiles for the kitchen, dining room and entrance cost £18 per square metre.
Work out the total cost of the floor tiles.

> **PROGRESS BAR** Colour in the progress bar as you get questions correct.
> Then fill in the progression chart on pages 111–113.

1 a Write down the name of each shape.

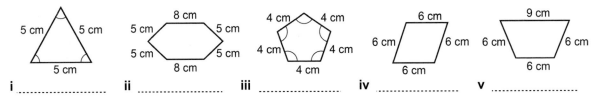

i ....   ii ....   iii ....   iv ....   v ....

   b Circle the quadrilaterals.   **c** Tick the regular polygons.

2 Work out the perimeter of this rectangle.

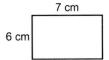

3 A regular hexagon has a side of 8 cm.
Work out its perimeter.

4 a Write down the order of rotational symmetry of each design.

i ....   ii ....   iii ....   iv ....   v ....

   b Draw the lines of symmetry on each design.

5 How many lines of symmetry does each shape in Q1 have?

i ....   ii ....   iii ....   iv ....   v ....

6 What is the area of the rectangle in Question 2?

7 The perimeter of this envelope is 64 cm.
Work out the height of the envelope.

22 cm

8 A regular octagon has a perimeter of 76 cm.
Work out the length of each side.

9 a Work out the perimeter of this shape.

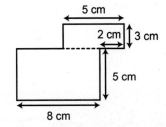

   b Work out the total area of the shape.

1 a Draw a line from each fraction to the correct shaded bar.

$\frac{4}{7}$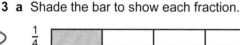

$\frac{2}{7}$

$\frac{5}{7}$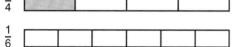

> A fraction is a part of a whole.

b Now write the fractions $\frac{4}{7}$, $\frac{2}{7}$ and $\frac{4}{7}$ in ascending order.

> **Literacy hint**
> Numbers in ascending order go from smallest to largest.

2 Write each set of fractions in ascending order.

a $\frac{5}{9}$ $\frac{2}{9}$ $\frac{8}{9}$ ································

b $\frac{9}{10}$ $\frac{3}{10}$ $\frac{7}{10}$ ································

> **Strategy hint**
> Draw and shade a diagram to help.

3 a Shade the bar to show each fraction.

Guided

$\frac{1}{4}$

$\frac{1}{6}$

> The number above the line in a fraction is the numerator. The number below the line is the denominator.
>
> $\frac{1}{2}$ ← numerator
> ← denominator

b Which is larger, $\frac{1}{4}$ or $\frac{1}{6}$? ·······················

c Two fractions have different denominators and a numerator of 1. How can you decide which is larger without drawing bars?

> Look at your answer to part **b**. Is the fraction with the larger denominator bigger or smaller than the other fraction?

4 Real Two games console websites are offering different discounts.

Website A: $\frac{1}{4}$ off all prices   Website B: $\frac{1}{5}$ off all prices

Which website is offering the better discount? Explain how you know.

5 Write the fraction of each shape that is shaded.

a   **b**   **c** 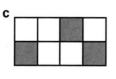 **d**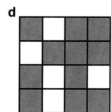

a ················
b ················
c ················
d ················
e ················
f ················
g ················
h ················

e   **f**   **g** 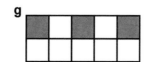 **h**

9.2 Equivalent fractions

Guided

1 Write these improper fractions as mixed numbers.

a $\frac{5}{3} = 1\frac{...}{3}$

b $\frac{7}{4}$ ----------

c $\frac{7}{6}$ ----------

d $\frac{12}{5}$ ----------

e $\frac{8}{3}$ ----------

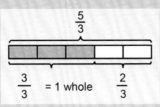

Three thirds make 1 whole. There are 2 thirds left over.

$\frac{5}{3}$

$\frac{3}{3}$ = 1 whole $\frac{2}{3}$

An improper fraction is a fraction in which the numerator is greater than the denominator.
A mixed number has a whole number part and a fraction part.
An improper fraction can be written as a mixed number.

2 Which of these fractions are equivalent? $\frac{3}{12}$ $\frac{3}{8}$ $\frac{2}{8}$

Equivalent fractions are fractions that represent the same amount but use different numerators and denominators.

$\frac{3}{12}$

$\frac{3}{8}$

$\frac{2}{8}$

Draw the fractions as bars, all the same length.

3 Circle the equivalent fractions

Draw the fractions as bars.

$\frac{3}{5}$ $\frac{3}{4}$ $\frac{4}{8}$ $\frac{6}{8}$ $\frac{9}{12}$

4 Simplify $\frac{3}{6}$

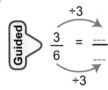

$\frac{3}{6} = \frac{...}{...}$ (÷3, ÷3)

Both 3 and 6 can be divided by 3, so divide the numerator and denominator by 3.

Multiplying or dividing the numerator and denominator by the same number gives an equivalent fraction. When the numerator and denominator are as small as possible, the fraction is simplified.
For example $\frac{2}{6} = \frac{1}{3}$ (÷2, ÷2)

5 Simplify these fractions.

a $\frac{6}{8} = \frac{...}{...}$ b $\frac{10}{15} = \frac{...}{...}$

c $\frac{30}{40} = \frac{...}{...}$ d $\frac{16}{20} = \frac{...}{...}$

e $\frac{12}{18} = \frac{...}{...}$ f $\frac{20}{30} = \frac{...}{...}$

Divide the numerator and denominator by the same number.

CHECK   Tick each box as your **confidence** in this topic improves.

Need extra help? Go to pages 97–98 and tick the boxes next to Q6, 10 and 11. Then have a go at them once you've finished 9.1–9.6.

1 Work out $\frac{1}{5}$ of 35.

$35 \div 5 =$ ....

How many in each $\frac{1}{5}$?

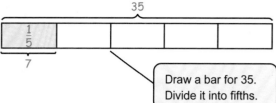

Draw a bar for 35. Divide it into fifths.

2 Work out

a $\frac{1}{4}$ of 36 .... **b** $\frac{1}{3}$ of 21 .... **c** $\frac{1}{5}$ of 40 .... **d** $\frac{1}{7}$ of 42 ....

e $\frac{1}{8}$ of 48 .... **f** $\frac{1}{10}$ of 90 .... **g** $\frac{1}{9}$ of 63 .... **h** $\frac{1}{6}$ of 24 ....

Use division to help you.

3 Find $\frac{1}{10}$ of

a 60 .... **b** 400 .... **c** 230 .... **d** 520 ....

e 27 .... **f** 66 .... **g** 362 .... **h** 428 ....

$27 \div 10 = 2.7$

4 Real / Finance The price of a pair of trainers is reduced by $\frac{1}{3}$ in a sale.

a Work out $\frac{1}{3}$ of £60. ....

b Work out the sale price of the trainers.

To find the sale price:
£60 $- \frac{1}{3}$ of £60 = ☐

5 A department store sells a pair of shoes for £37.
It reduces its prices by $\frac{1}{10}$ in a sale.

a Work out $\frac{1}{10}$ of £37. ....

b Work out the sale price of the shoes.

c Work out the sale price of each of these items.

£26

£49

£12

6 Real Two shops offer different deals on bikes.
Which shop has the cheaper bike?

Shop A

USUALLY £190 NOW $\frac{1}{10}$ OFF

Shop B

£220 REDUCED BY $\frac{1}{4}$

CHECK Tick each box as your **confidence** in this topic improves.

Need extra help? Go to page 97 and tick the boxes next to Q4 and 5. Then have a go at them once you've finished 9.1–9.6.

9.4 Adding and subtracting fractions

1 Work out $\frac{1}{5} + \frac{2}{5}$

Guided

$\frac{1}{5} + \frac{3}{5} =$ ....

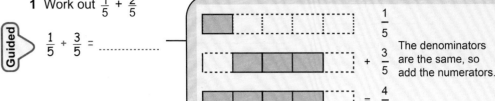

$\frac{1}{5}$

$+ \frac{3}{5}$ The denominators are the same, so add the numerators.

$= \frac{4}{5}$

Fractions with a common denominator have the same denominator.

2 Work out

a $\frac{2}{5} + \frac{1}{5}$ .... **b** $\frac{3}{10} + \frac{4}{10}$ .... **c** $\frac{5}{9} + \frac{2}{9}$ .... **d** $\frac{2}{15} + \frac{9}{15}$ ....

3 Work out $\frac{7}{8} - \frac{4}{8}$

Guided

$\frac{7}{8} - \frac{4}{8} =$ ....

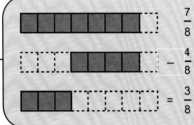

$\frac{7}{8}$

$- \frac{4}{8}$ The denominators are the same, so subtract the numerators.

$= \frac{3}{8}$

4 Work out

a $\frac{5}{7} - \frac{2}{7}$ .... **b** $\frac{9}{10} - \frac{2}{10}$ .... **c** $\frac{5}{9} - \frac{1}{9}$ .... **d** $\frac{3}{6} - \frac{2}{6}$ ....

5 Work out $\frac{4}{5} + \frac{3}{5}$. Write your answer as a mixed number.

Guided

$\frac{4}{5} + \frac{3}{5} = \frac{\cdots}{5} = 1\frac{\cdots}{5}$

A mixed number has a whole number part and a fraction part.

For example, $1\frac{3}{10}$ is a mixed number.

6 Work out

a $\frac{5}{6} + \frac{2}{6}$ .... **b** $\frac{4}{7} + \frac{5}{7}$ .... **c** $\frac{7}{10} + \frac{6}{10}$ .... **d** $\frac{5}{9} + \frac{8}{9}$ ....

7 Work out $1 - \frac{3}{5}$

Guided

$1 - \frac{3}{5} = \frac{5}{5} - \frac{3}{5} = \frac{\cdots}{5}$ $\boxed{1 = \frac{5}{5}}$

When the numerator and denominator are the same, the fraction equals one whole.

8 Work out

a $1 - \frac{4}{7}$ .... **b** $1 - \frac{1}{6}$ .... **c** $1 - \frac{3}{10}$ .... **d** $1 - \frac{7}{12}$ ....

9 Freya cuts a pizza into 8 slices.
She eats 2 slices and her friend Dan eats 3 slices.

a What fraction of the pizza have they eaten altogether?

b What fraction of the pizza is left?

1 pizza $= \frac{\square}{8}$

Worked example

CHECK Tick each box as your **confidence** in this topic improves.

94

Need extra help? Go to pages 97–98 and tick the boxes next to Q7, 8 and 9. Then have a go at them once you've finished 9.1–9.6.

1 What percentage of the grid is shaded?

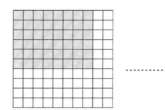

............%

Guided

> Per cent means 'out of 100'.
> '%' stands for 'per cent'.

> There are 100 squares.
> 48 out of 100 squares are shaded.

2 Finance   A bank account pays £3 interest on savings of £100.

What percentage is this? ....

3 Write 60% as a fraction in its simplest form.

Guided

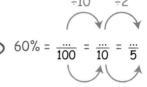

$60\% = \frac{...}{100} = \frac{...}{10} = \frac{...}{5}$

> First write 60% as a fraction of 100.

> Then simplify the fraction by dividing the numerator and denominator by the same number. Keep doing this until the fraction is in its simplest form.

4 Write these percentages as fractions in their simplest form.

a 27% ....   **b** 61% ....   **c** 10% ....   **d** 40% ....

5 Write these percentages as decimals.

Guided

a 32%

> Write 32% as a fraction out of 100. Then divide 32 by 100 to write it as a decimal.

$32\% = \frac{...}{100} = $ ....

b 19% ....   **c** 63% ....   **d** 54% ....   **e** 6% ....

6 Write these percentages as fractions and as decimals.

Guided

a $50\% = \frac{...}{100} = \frac{...}{2}$ $50\% = 0.50 = $ ....   **b** $10\% = \frac{...}{100} = \frac{...}{10}$ $10\% = $ ....

c $20\% = \frac{...}{100} = \frac{...}{5}$ $20\% = $ ....   **d** $1\% = \frac{...}{100}$ $1\% = $ ....

7 Draw lines to match each percentage and its equivalent fraction.

30%   20%   75%   70%   4%   49%

$\frac{1}{25}$ $\frac{7}{10}$ $\frac{49}{100}$ $\frac{1}{5}$ $\frac{3}{10}$ $\frac{3}{4}$

8 Finance   Two music download websites offer different discounts.

Website A: 30% off all prices   Website B: $\frac{1}{10}$ off all prices

a Write 30% as a fraction. ....

b Which website offers the better discount? ....

Worked example

CHECK   Tick each box as your **confidence** in this topic improves.

Need extra help? Go to page 98 and tick the boxes next to Q12 and 13. Then have a go at them once you've finished 9.1–9.6.

1 Find 50% of

   a 60 ....   **b** 24 ....

   c 86 ....   **d** 136 ....

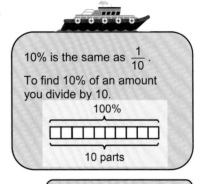

50% is the same as $\frac{1}{2}$.

To find 50% of an amount you divide by 2.

100%

1 whole

2 **Finance**   A mobile phone tariff increases by 50%. It was £25 per month.

   a How much does it increase by? ....

   b What is the monthly price now? ....

3 Find 10% of

   a 300 ....   **b** 70 ....   **c** 172 ....

4 **Finance**   A bank pays 10% interest on all its accounts each year. How much interest would each of these amounts earn in a year?

   a £2000 ....   **b** £1600 ....

   c £340 ....   **d** £247 ....

10% is the same as $\frac{1}{10}$.

To find 10% of an amount you divide by 10.

100%

10 parts

5 Find 1% of

   a 500

   500 ÷ 100

   = ...

$1\% = \frac{1}{100}$

So to find 1%, divide 500 by 100.

To find 1% of an amount you divide by 100.

   b 200 ....   **c** 320 ....   **d** 2000 ....

   e 124 ....   **f** 253 ....   **g** 82 ....

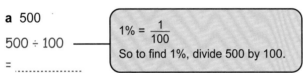

Guided

6 **Finance**   A director of a company decides to give his staff a 1% pay rise. The table shows the salaries earned each year. Work out each person's pay rise, and complete the table.

Employee	Mr Beech	Miss Khan	Mrs Payne	Mr Shaw	Mr Thornton
Salary	£27 000	£30 000	£18 000	£41 000	£22 000
Increase					

7 **Real / Finance**   In 2013 cocoa beans from India cost on average £1700 per ton. The price rose by 10% at the start of 2014. How much did cocoa beans cost in 2014?

CHECK   Tick each box as your **confidence** in this topic improves.

Need extra help? Go to page 98 and tick the boxes next to Q14–18. Then have a go at them once you've finished 9.1–9.6.

1 Circle the largest fraction in each set of three.

> Which bar has the largest area shaded?

a $\frac{7}{10}$

b $\frac{5}{9}$

$\frac{9}{10}$

$\frac{2}{9}$

$\frac{3}{10}$

$\frac{8}{9}$

2 Look at the bars. Circle the larger fraction in each set.

a $\frac{1}{10}$

b $\frac{1}{3}$

$\frac{1}{4}$

$\frac{1}{7}$

3 Circle the larger fraction in each pair.

> You could draw bars to help you. Make the two bars the same length.

a $\frac{1}{4}$ or $\frac{1}{3}$ **b** $\frac{1}{5}$ or $\frac{1}{7}$ **c** $\frac{1}{9}$ or $\frac{1}{2}$

> Draw a bar to show 63.
> Divide it into sevenths.
> Work out how many in one part.
> 63
> $\frac{1}{7}$

Guided

4 Find $\frac{1}{7}$ of 63

$63 \div 7 =$ _____

> How many in each $\frac{1}{7}$?

5 Use the bars to find   Work out how many in one part.

a $\frac{1}{4}$ of 24   **b** $\frac{1}{10}$ of 70.

_____   _____

6 Complete these to simplify the fractions.

a $\div 3$

$\frac{15}{18} = \frac{\dots}{6}$

$\div 3$

b $\div 10$

$\frac{40}{70} = \frac{4}{\dots}$

$\div 10$

c $\div 7$

$\frac{21}{28} = \frac{\dots}{\dots}$

$\div 7$

d $\div \dots$

$\frac{35}{50} = \frac{\dots}{10}$

$\div \dots$

7 Use the bars to work out

> Shade in two ninths and three ninths. How much is shaded altogether?

a $\frac{2}{9} + \frac{3}{9}$ _____

> Read out loud, 'two ninths add three ninths is ☐ ninths.'

b $\frac{1}{10} + \frac{6}{10}$ _____

c $\frac{4}{11} + \frac{5}{11}$ _____

d $\frac{5}{15} + \frac{6}{15}$ _____

8 Complete these calculations.

a $\frac{5}{7} - \frac{2}{7} = \frac{\dots}{7}$ **b** $\frac{7}{10} - \frac{4}{10} = \frac{\dots}{10}$ **c** $\frac{8}{9} - \frac{3}{9} = \frac{\dots}{9}$

> Read out loud, 'five sevenths take away two sevenths is ☐ sevenths.'

9 Work out

a $1 - \frac{1}{3}$ .... **b** $1 - \frac{3}{7}$ .... **c** $1 - \frac{2}{9}$ .... **d** $1 - \frac{7}{10}$ ....

$1 = \frac{3}{3}$

$\frac{1}{3}$ $\frac{1}{3}$ $\frac{1}{3}$

10 $\frac{7}{4}$ of these bars are shaded.

a How many whole bars are shaded? ....

b Complete: $\frac{7}{4} = 1\frac{....}{4}$

11 Use the bars to show $\frac{7}{5}$

$\frac{7}{5} = 1\frac{....}{5}$

Worked example

Equivalent fractions, decimals and percentages

12 Write these percentages as fractions.

Guided

a $27\% = \frac{....}{100}$ **b** $61\% = \frac{....}{100}$ **c** 17% .... **d** 37% ....

13 Write these percentages as fractions and then simplify the fraction.

a

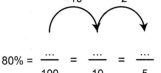

$80\% = \frac{...}{100} = \frac{...}{10} = \frac{...}{5}$

b

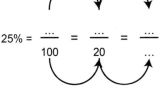

$25\% = \frac{...}{100} = \frac{...}{20} = \frac{...}{...}$

c

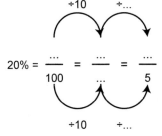

$20\% = \frac{...}{100} = \frac{...}{...} = \frac{...}{5}$

Finding percentages

14 **a** What do you divide by to find 50%? ....

Guided

b Work out 50% of 58.

$58 \div .... = ...$

58
| 50% | 50% |
___ ___

15 Find 50% of

a £40 .... **b** £160 .... **c** £260 ....

d £190 .... **e** £350 .... **f** £15 ....

16 **a** What do you divide by to find 10%? ....

b Work out 10% of 80. ....

100%
|10%|10%|10%|10%|10%|10%|10%|10%|10%|10%|
___ parts

17 Find 10% of

a 70 .... **b** 600 .... **c** 170 ....

d 150 .... **e** 730 .... **f** 67 ....

18 Find 1% of

a 700 .... **b** 1600 .... **c** 1200 .... **d** 350 ....

To find 1% divide by 100.

1 Finance   A teacher records what fraction of her budget she spends on resources.

$\frac{1}{12}$ Paint $\frac{1}{5}$ Paper $\frac{1}{3}$ Books $\frac{1}{10}$ Pens and pencils

What does the teacher spend the most money on from this list? ....

2 100 people were asked which was their favourite potato product.

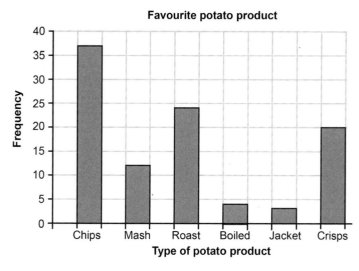

Favourite potato product

a What percentage of people liked jacket potatoes best? ....

b What fraction of people liked

   i chips best ....

   ii crisps best ....

   iii mash or boiled potatoes best? ....

   Give your answers as fractions in their simplest form.

> How many people altogether liked mash best or boiled potatoes best?

3 a What is 10% of 243? ....

  b What is 20% of 243? ....

> To work out 20%, find 10% and multiply by ☐

4 Work out 20% of

  a £210 ....   **b** £452 ....   **c** 137 cm ....   **d** 326 km ....

Guided

10% of £210 = ...

20% of £210 = ...

5 Work out

  a 30% of 340   **b** 60% of 230

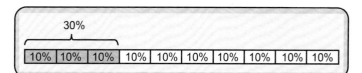

30%

| 10% | 10% | 10% | 10% | 10% | 10% | 10% | 10% | 10% | 10% |

  c 40% of 650   **d** 70% of 130

Worked example

  e 90% of 520   **f** 80% of 190

6 Finance Phone prices are reduced by 30% in a sale. A smartphone costs £540.

   a Work out 30% of £540.

   b What is the sale price of the phone?

7 A competition offers the following prizes.

   50% of £150 $\frac{1}{4}$ of £320 $\frac{1}{6}$ of £450

   Which prize is worth the most? Show your workings.

8 a Draw lines to join the cards into sets of three equivalent values.

$\frac{9}{20}$ $\frac{75}{100}$ $\frac{99}{100}$ $\frac{13}{100}$ $\frac{1}{50}$ $\frac{31}{100}$ $\frac{1}{5}$

13% 20% 31% 2% 45% 99% 75%

0.31 0.7 0.45 0.13 0.75 0.2 0.02 0.99

   b Which card does not have any equivalent cards to match to? ....

   c Write two other cards to complete the set for the odd one out.

9 STEM An elephant calf usually gains 50% of its birth weight after 4 weeks.
A newly born elephant calf weighs 138 kg. How much should it weigh after 4 weeks?

10 Which is greater, $\frac{2}{5}$ of £260 or $\frac{1}{3}$ of £309?

> To work out $\frac{2}{5}$, work out $\frac{1}{5}$
> and multiply by ☐

11 Problem-solving Write a list of 12 numbers so that 50% of them are
even, $\frac{1}{4}$ of them are multiples of 7 and $\frac{1}{6}$ of them are larger than 100.

> Work out how many of
> each type of number you
> need.
> 50% of 12 = ☐

PROGRESS BAR Colour in the progress bar as you get questions correct.
Then fill in the progression chart on pages 111–113.

1 Write these fractions in order from smallest to largest.

$\frac{6}{11}, \frac{3}{11}, \frac{9}{11}, \frac{5}{11}, \frac{10}{11}$ ....

2 a What fraction of each shape is shaded?

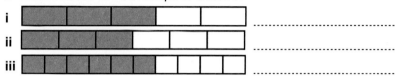

i ....

ii ....

iii ....

b Which two fractions in part a are equivalent? ....

3 Work out

a $\frac{1}{4}$ of 20 .... b $\frac{1}{3}$ of 30 .... c $\frac{1}{2}$ of 38 .... d $\frac{1}{5}$ of 40 ....

4 Write down the number that makes each sentence correct.

a To find $\frac{1}{6}$ you divide by ....

b Calculating $\frac{1}{8}$ is the same as dividing by ....

5 In a test of 100 questions, Shane answered 67 questions correctly.

What percentage did he get? ....

6 Work out

a 50% of 140 .... b 10% of 60 .... c 10% of 200 .... d 1% of 700 ....

7 Everything is reduced by 10% in a sale. The original price of a pair of jeans was £30.

a Work out 10% of £30. ....

b What is the sale price of the jeans? ....

8 Convert these percentages to fractions.

a 23% = $\frac{....}{100}$ b 30% = $\frac{....}{100} = \frac{....}{10}$ c 20% = $\frac{....}{100} = \frac{....}{10} = \frac{....}{5}$

9 Write these percentages as decimals.

a 47% .... b 96% .... c 40% .... d 5% ....

10 Work out

a $\frac{2}{5} + \frac{2}{5}$ .... b $\frac{2}{7} + \frac{3}{7} + \frac{1}{7}$ .... c $\frac{5}{7} + \frac{2}{7}$ .... d $1 - \frac{2}{5}$ ....

11 Change these improper fractions to mixed numbers.

a $\frac{7}{4} = 1\frac{....}{....}$ b $\frac{4}{3} = ...\frac{....}{....}$ c $\frac{10}{7} = ...\frac{....}{....}$

12 Work out $\frac{4}{7} + \frac{4}{7} + \frac{3}{7}$.

Give your answer as a mixed number. ....

10.1 Reflection

1 Which is the correct reflection of each shape in its mirror line?

a ....3........

b ....

c ....

d ....

e ....

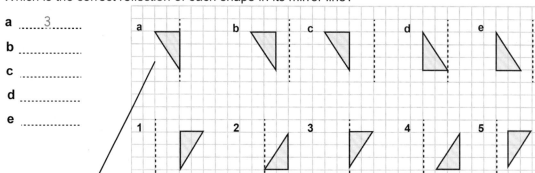

Shape A looks like shapes 1, 3 and 5 when it is reflected in a mirror. Shapes A and 3 are touching the mirror line (shape 1 is two squares away from the mirror line and shape 5 is one square away).

A reflection is a type of transformation. When a shape or object is reflected in a mirror the shape 'flips' over.

2 Reflect each shape in its mirror line.

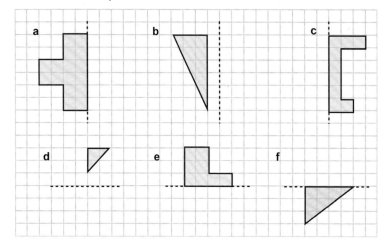

All points on an object are the same distance from a mirror line as the points on the image, but on the opposite side.

3 a Draw in the mirror line for each pair of shapes.

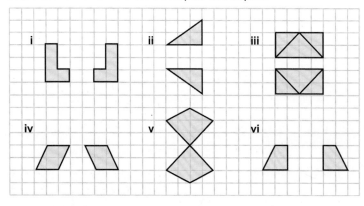

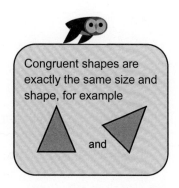

Congruent shapes are exactly the same size and shape, for example

and

b Are the shapes in each pair congruent? ....

Need extra help? Go to page 106 and tick the boxes next to Q1 and 2. Then have a go at them once you've finished 10.1–10.4.

1 Describe each translation.

a A to B ....

b A to C ....

c E to F ....

d A to D ....

e B to E ....

f C to G ....

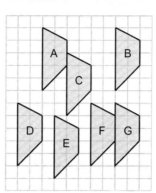

A translation is a type of transformation. A translation moves a shape across a surface.
Describe a translation as a movement left or right, then up or down.

First give moves left or right, then up or down.
A to C: ☐ squares right and ☐ squares down.

2 Translate the shape 4 squares right and 3 squares up.

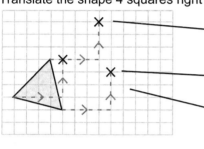

Choose one of the corners and translate it 4 right, 3 up.

Repeat this for the other corners.

Join up the 3 translated corners, using straight lines.

Worked example

3 Translate these shapes.

a 6 right

b 3 down

c 3 right, 4 down

d 5 right, 2 up

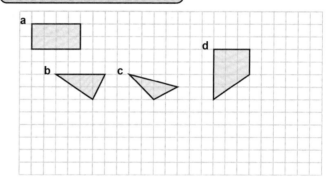

4 Write down the coordinates of the cross after each translation.

a 3 left ....

b 5 down ....

c 2 right, 4 up ....

d 3 left, 5 up ....

e 4 right, 3 down ....

f 2 left, 4 down ....

g 5 left, 3 up ....

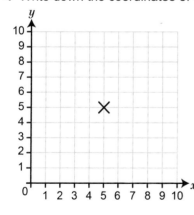

5 Translate shape A

a 4 squares right. Label it B.

b 5 squares down. Label it C.

c 2 squares right, 3 squares down. Label it D.

d 5 squares right, 4 squares down. Label it E.

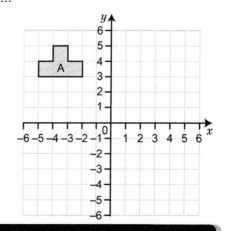

CHECK Tick each box as your **confidence** in this topic improves.

Need extra help? Go to page 106 and tick the boxes next to Q3 and 4. Then have a go at them once you've finished 10.1–10.4.

1 a Circle the shapes which have been rotated through a $\frac{1}{4}$ turn.

  b Tick the shapes which have been rotated through a $\frac{1}{2}$ turn.

> Turning a shape through an angle is called a rotation. A rotation is a type of transformation.

A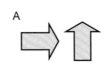

B

C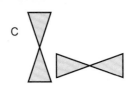

D

E

F

2 Circle the shapes which are rotations of shape A.

> Trace shape A and see if it will fit exactly over the images.

 A
 B
 C
 D E
 F

3 Rotate these shapes.

a $\frac{1}{4}$ turn anticlockwise   **b** $\frac{1}{2}$ turn   **c** $\frac{1}{4}$ turn clockwise   **d** $\frac{1}{4}$ turn anticlockwise

a

> Rotate the tracing paper through a $\frac{1}{4}$ turn anticlockwise.

> Draw the shape in its new position.

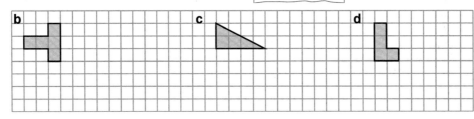

4 Rotate each shape through the angle given about the centre of rotation marked ×.

> Use tracing paper to help you.

a 180°   **b** 90° clockwise   **c** 90° anticlockwise

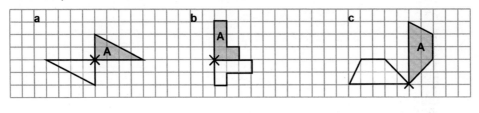

5 Each shape marked A has been rotated about the centre of rotation ×. Describe each rotation.

> Give the angle and direction.

 a **b** **c**

....

....

CHECK   Tick each box as your **confidence** in this topic improves.

Need extra help? Go to pages 106 and 107 and tick the boxes next to Q5–8. Then have a go at them once you've finished 10.1–10.4.

1 STEM A computer programmer is working on a game where shapes fit together.

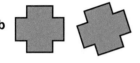
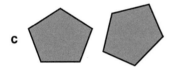

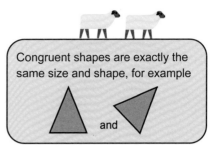

Congruent shapes are exactly the same size and shape, for example

and

Which shapes are congruent? ....

2 Reasoning Are these pairs of shapes congruent? Give a reason for your answer.

Use tracing paper to check the shapes are the same size and shape.

 Guided

a

No, because ....

Trace the shape.

b

....

c

....

3 Which two of these triangles are congruent? Explain how you know.

 A　　　　 B　　　　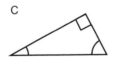 C

....

4 Are these pairs of shapes congruent? Explain how you know.

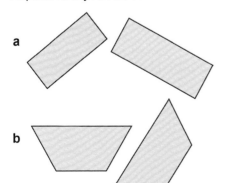

a

....

....

b

....

....

....

CHECK　Tick each box as your **confidence** in this topic improves.

Need extra help? Go to page 108 and tick the box next to Q9. Then have a go at it once you've finished 10.1–10.4.

105

Reflection

1 Circle the reflections which have the mirror line in the correct place.

> Count the squares from each corner on the shape to the mirror line.

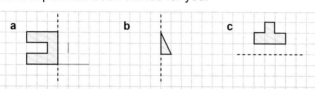

2 Reflect the shapes in the mirror lines.
The first part has been started for you.

> The reflection must be the same size as the original shape.

Guided

Translation

3 For each diagram, describe how shape A moves to shape B.

a ....

b ....

c ....

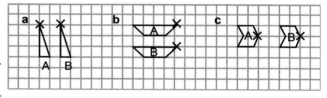

4 a Which two of triangles A–D are translations of the shaded triangle?

....

b Describe the two translations.

....

....

> A translation is a slide. A translated shape is exactly the same shape and size and is the same way round.

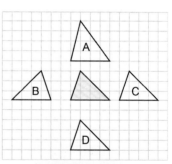

Rotation

5 Are these shapes rotated $\frac{1}{4}$ turn or $\frac{1}{2}$ turn?

> Turning your book upside down would involve a $\frac{1}{2}$ turn.

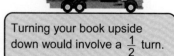

a

b

c

....

d

e

f

....

106

6 All the shaded shapes have been rotated $\frac{1}{4}$ turn. Write clockwise or anticlockwise for each one.

a ....

b ....

c ....

d ....

anticlockwise   clockwise

7 **a** Trace this triangle. Turn the tracing a $\frac{1}{2}$ turn.
Now draw the rotation.

b Repeat for a $\frac{1}{4}$ turn clockwise.

c Repeat for a $\frac{3}{4}$ turn anticlockwise.

d What do you notice about **b** and **c**?

8 The shaded shapes have been rotated about a centre of rotation marked ×. Describe each rotation.

What is this angle?

a ....° anticlockwise

b ....

c ....

90°   180°   270°

Congruency

9 Which of these pairs of shapes are congruent? ....

A

B

Trace one of the pair.
If the tracing fits exactly
over the other shape,
then they are congruent.

C

D

1 a Describe the translation that takes this shape from

    i A to B ....

    ii B to A. ....

  b What do you notice about your answers to part **a**?

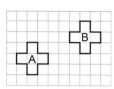

2 This shape is translated 4 squares right and 3 squares up.
It is then translated 3 squares left and 2 squares down.

  a Draw the image after each of the translations.

  b What translation takes the original shape to the final image?

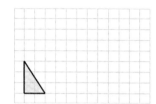

3 The diagram shows four triangles on a coordinate grid.
Write whether each statement is true or false.

  a A translation from A to B is 4 right, 1 down. ....

  b A translation from D to C is 4 left, 1 up. ....

  c A translation from A to D is 6 down. ....

  d A translation from C to A is 5 left, 5 up. ....

  e All the triangles have the same area. ....

  f The triangles do not have the same perimeter. ....

Guided

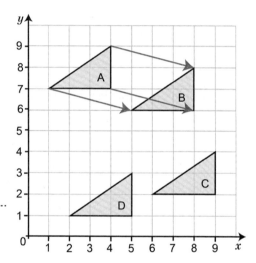

4 Which of these logos are exactly the same when

  a translated 5 units left and 3 units up ....

  b rotated through a $\frac{1}{2}$ turn clockwise ....

  c reflected in a horizontal line? ....

A horizontal line runs across the page.

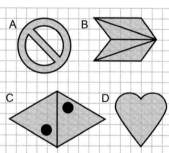

5 Circle the congruent triangles.

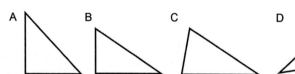

6 Write whether each statement is true or false.

  a When you rotate a shape, the image is *not* congruent. ....

  b When you translate a shape, the image is congruent. ....

  c When you reflect a shape, the image is *not* congruent. ....

  d The areas of two congruent shapes are equal. ....

  e When you translate a triangle, the image always looks identical to the original. ....

  f When you reflect a triangle, the image always looks identical to the original. ....

  g When you rotate a triangle through a $\frac{1}{2}$ turn, the image always

    looks identical to the original. ....

7 The points A–G are reflected in the mirror line shown. Write the coordinates of the image of each point.

A ....

B ....

C ....

D ....

E ....

F ....

G ....

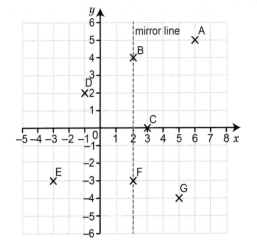

8 a Points B, C and D are translations of point A. Mark them on the grid.

    B 3 left

    C 7 left, 5 down

    D 2 right, 5 down

b Join the points in the order A, B, C, D, A.

c Name this shape. ....

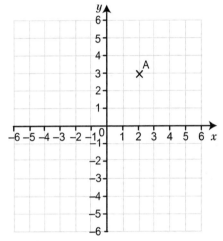

9 Becky plots the point (3, −5) on a coordinate grid. She then translates it 8 up, 5 left, then 3 down, 7 right.

   a What are the coordinates of the new point? ....

   b What transformation will take it back to (3, −5)?

Strategy hint
Draw out a coordinate grid and mark on the points.

10 a Reflect shape A in the mirror line. Label the image B.

   b Translate shape B 4 right and 3 down. Label the image C.

   c Describe a translation that moves C to A.

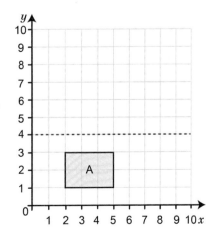

Worked example

10 Unit test

1 The shaded arrow has been translated 2 right and 3 down.

Which is the correct image? ....

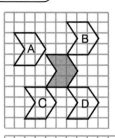

2 Which shape is triangle T after

a $\frac{1}{2}$ turn .... **b** $\frac{1}{4}$ turn clockwise ....

c $\frac{1}{4}$ turn anticlockwise? ....

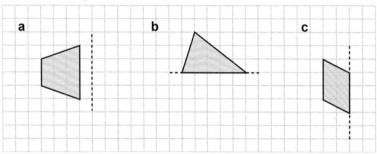

3 Reflect the shapes in the mirror lines shown.

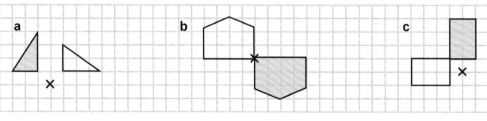

4 The shaded shapes have been rotated about the centre of rotation ×.
Describe each rotation.

    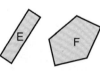

....

5 Which pairs of shapes are congruent? ....

6 Explain why these two triangles are not congruent.

7 Use the centre of rotation ×. Rotate the shaded shape

a 90° anticlockwise. Label it A.

b 90° clockwise. Label it B.

c 180°. Label it C.

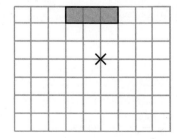

Progression charts

Progression is all about checking your confidence in the maths that you're learning.
- For each Unit test, tick the questions you answered correctly.
- Then rate your confidence by ticking a smiley face.

1 Analysing and displaying data

I can...	Unit 1: Unit test
Interpret data in tables, charts and diagrams and record data in a frequency table.	Q1 ☐ Q2 ☐
Find the modal class for grouped data and find the mode, range, median and mean of a set of data.	Q3 ☐ Q4 ☐
My confidence	☹ ☐ 😐 ☐ 🙂 ☐

2 Calculating

I can...	Unit 2: Unit test
Add and subtract numbers in different ways.	Q1 ☐ Q3 ☐ Q6 ☐ Q7 ☐ Q9 ☐
Solve simple ratio and proportion problems.	Q5 ☐ Q13 ☐
Round and approximate numbers.	Q8 ☐
Multiply numbers and recognise multiples and square numbers.	Q4 ☐ Q11 ☐
Multiply and divide by 10, 100 and 1000.	Q12 ☐
Use simple negative numbers.	Q2 ☐ Q10 ☐
My confidence	☹ ☐ 😐 ☐ 🙂 ☐

3 Expressions, functions and formulae

I can...	Unit 3: Unit test
Find outputs of and describe simple functions.	Q1 ☐ Q2 ☐
Simplify expressions by collecting like terms.	Q3 ☐
Write expressions from a description in words and write simple formulae using letter symbols.	Q4 ☐ Q6 ☐ Q9 ☐
Substitute integers into simple formulae expressed in words or letter symbols.	Q5 ☐ Q7 ☐ Q8 ☐
My confidence	☹ ☐ 😐 ☐ 🙂 ☐

4 Graphs

I can...	Unit 4: Unit test
Read x- and y-coordinates and information from a real-life graph.	Q1 ☐ Q3 ☐

Plot coordinates and graphs of simple functions.	Q2 ☐

My confidence ☹ ☐ 😐 ☐ 🙂 ☐

5 Factors and multiples

I can...	Unit 5: Unit test
Use the priority of operations.	Q4 ☐
Multiply and divide 3-digit numbers by a single digit.	Q2 ☐ Q10 ☐
Recognise and use multiples and factors and apply simple tests of divisibility.	Q1 ☐ Q3 ☐ Q5 ☐
Find common factors, primes, HCF and LCM.	Q6 ☐ Q7 ☐ Q8 ☐ Q9 ☐

My confidence ☹ ☐ 😐 ☐ 🙂 ☐

6 Decimals and measures

I can...	Unit 6: Unit test
Read a variety of scales.	Q1 ☐ Q2 ☐
Draw and measure lines to the nearest millimetre (in mm).	Q3 ☐
Know the value of each digit in a number.	Q4 ☐
Convert and order metric measurements.	Q9 ☐ Q10 ☐
Add, subtract and order decimal numbers.	Q5 ☐ Q6 ☐ Q7 ☐ Q8 ☐
Round decimals to one decimal place or to the nearest whole number.	Q11 ☐ Q12 ☐
Enter and interpret numbers on a calculator (decimals and money).	Q13 ☐

My confidence ☹ ☐ 😐 ☐ 🙂 ☐

7 Angles and lines

I can...	Unit 7: Unit test
Identify right angles, perpendicular and parallel lines as well as acute, obtuse and reflex angles.	Q1 ☐ Q2 ☐ Q3 ☐ Q4 ☐
Label lines and angles correctly.	Q5 ☐
Use a protractor to draw acute angles to the nearest degree.	Q6 ☐
Know the sum of angles on a straight line and round a point.	Q7 ☐

My confidence ☹ ☐ 😐 ☐ 🙂 ☐

8 Measuring and shapes

I can...	Unit 8: Unit test
Give the names of regular polygons.	Q1 ☐
Calculate perimeters of rectangles and regular polygons and solve problems involving them.	Q2 ☐ Q3 ☐ Q8 ☐ Q9 ☐
Calculate the perimeter and area of shapes made from rectangles.	Q6 ☐
Use a formulae to calculate the area of squares and rectangles.	Q7 ☐
Describe the symmetry of triangles and other shapes.	Q4 ☐ Q5 ☐
My confidence ☹ ☐ 😐 ☐ 🙂 ☐	

9 Fractions, decimals and percentages

I can...	Unit 9: Unit test
Identify equivalent fractions and relate fractions to division and parts of shapes.	Q2 ☐ Q4 ☐
Change an improper fraction to a mixed number.	Q11 ☐
Find simple fractions and simple percentages of whole number quantities.	Q3 ☐ Q6 ☐
Add, subtract and order simple fractions.	Q1 ☐ Q10 ☐ Q12 ☐
Understand a percentage as the number of parts per 100 and convert a percentage to a number of hundredths or tenths.	Q5 ☐ Q7 ☐
Write a percentage as a fraction or decimal.	Q8 ☐ Q9 ☐
My confidence ☹ ☐ 😐 ☐ 🙂 ☐	

10 Transformations

I can...	Unit 10: Unit test
Understand reflections and reflect a shape in a mirror line.	Q3 ☐
Understand translation and translate a shape.	Q1 ☐
Understand, draw and describe rotations.	Q2 ☐ Q4 ☐ Q7 ☐
Understand the term 'congruent' and identify congruent shapes.	Q5 ☐ Q6 ☐
My confidence ☹ ☐ 😐 ☐ 🙂 ☐	

Progress with confidence

Our innovative Progression Workbooks are focussed on building your confidence in maths and let you take control of your learning.

- Chart how well you're doing against specific Learning Objectives with Progression Charts for each Unit
- Keep track of your strengths and weaknesses with Confidence Checkers at the end of each lesson and Unit
- Take control of your work and progression with loads of write-in practice

The Workbooks also offer plenty of dynamic support to help build your confidence in maths.

- Get direct access to worked example videos on your phone or tablet using the QR codes, providing crucial support for tricky questions
- Help structure your answers with guided questions and partially worked solutions
- Break down any barriers to learning with hints and key learning points for each topic

Delivering the 2014 National Curriculum

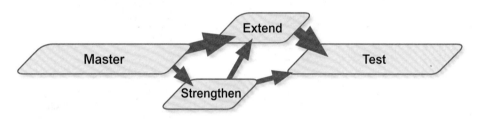

Progress with confidence with hundreds of extra practice questions for Fluency, Problem-solving and Reasoning, as well as Modelling, Finance, Real and STEM.

Other components include: Student Books and **ActiveLearn** Digital Service.

For more information visit www.pearsonschools.co.uk/ks3mathsprogress

www.pearsonschools.co.uk | **T** 0845 630 33 33
myorders@pearson.com | **F** 0845 630 77 77

ISBN 978-1-4479-7111-5

9 781447 971115